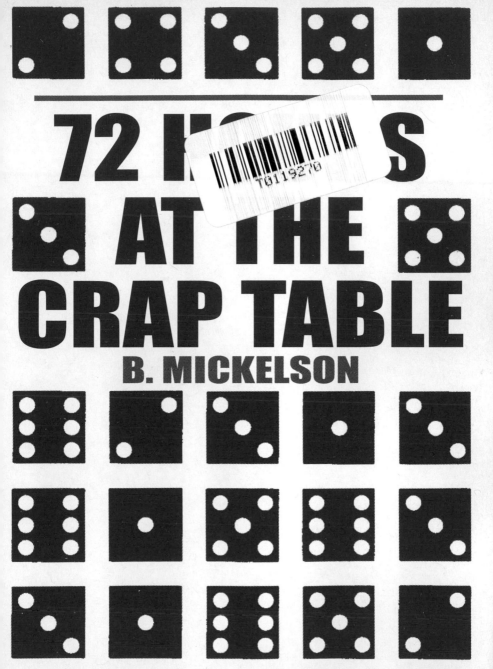

72 HOURS AT THE CRAP TABLE

B. MICKELSON

This underground craps classic outlines 72 straight hours at the craps table faithfully recording every single roll, streak, win, play, and loss in actual game action—a must for systems players who need real results to test their systems.

72 HOURS
AT THE
CRAP TABLE
B. MICKELSON

GBC PRESS
P. O. Box 98115
Las Vegas, NV 89193
www.gamblersbookclub.com

GBC Press books are published by Gambler's Books Club in Las Vegas, Nevada. Since 1964, the legendary GBC has been the reigning authority on gambling publications and the only dedicated gambling bookstore in the world.

Copyright © 1979, 2015 by Gamblers Book Club
All Rights Reserved

This is a revised edition of the classic republished by GBC Press in the 1970s

Library of Congress Catalog Number: 2015935844
ISBN 10: 1-58042-330-2   ISBN 13: 978-1-58042-330-4
GBC Press is an imprint of Cardoza Publishing

GBC PRESS
c/o Cardoza Publishing
P.O. Box 98115, Las Vegas, NV 89193
Toll-Free Phone (800)522-1777
email: info@gamblersbookclub.com
www.gamblersbookclub.com

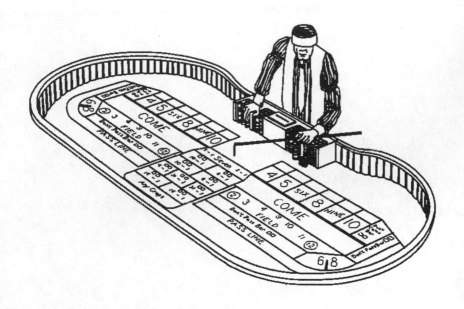

TABLE OF CONTENTS

72 HOURS AT THE CRAP TABLE

HOW TO USE THIS BOOK

Anyone with a system for beating the crap table will be wise to test and retest before going into live action. The accepted opinion is that the perfect system will never be found but when gambling at casino games some system, method or plan is essential. To play indiscriminately is a sure way to loose one's money. Equally important is that the game is much more interesting when thoroughly understood and really becomes a challenge when some form of money management is used to overcome the negative expectation.

With some definite wagering plan follow the actual rolls of the dice to test the result of your "system." To go through the entire book simulates a three day siege at the table and is a good test, but not conclusive. Any plan that shows promise should be tested further at low minimum tables before any serious playing is considered.

The numbers are true recordings of crap table rolls. Each line is a new shooter and an indented line is the continuation of the same shooter. The hardway 4, 6, 8 and 10 are printed in bold type. The first line on page 1 reads -- "The shooter came out with a hard 6 (3-3), then rolled 10, 3, 2 and a loser 7. The next line is the next shooter who came out with a 6 easy way (4-2 or 5-1), and the the very next roll a loser 7. A new shooter on line 3 came out with a crap 3 which loses. His next come out roll was a natural 7, a winner, then a point 10 which he made the next roll; then another crap (12) which loses again. He came out with easy 6, rolled 4 and then a loser 7 to complete his hand.

The right side of the page repeats each player's hand in abbreviated form. O Missout, X Pass, C Craps, B Crap 12, and 2 Crap 2. The third line reads Crap 3, Pass, Pass, Crap 12 and a Missout.

The line at the bottom of each page repeats the pass-missout decisions in graph form, the small o's being passes and the squares missouts. The come out rolls of 12 are indicated by the blackened squares.

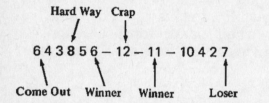

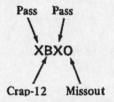

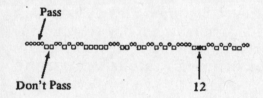

RECAP OF 72 HOURS AT THE CRAPS TABLE

Shooters 1829   Total Rolls 14,967   Decisions 4525

Pass Line Winners 2152   Come Out Roll   Don't Pass Winners 2244

                          of 12 129

Pass Line Losers   2373   Don't Pass Losers   2152

Point	2	3	4	5	6	7	8	9	10	11	12
Actual Rolls	401	853	1236	1668	2008	2574	2081	1601	1253	875	417
Theory Rolls	416	832	1248	1664	2080	2496	2080	1664	1248	832	416

Runs-Pass Line	1	2	3	4	5	6	7	8	9	10	11	12	13
	613	282	121	69	30	16	4	1	0	3	1	0	1

Runs-Don't Pass	1	2	3	4	5	6	7	8	9	10	11
	552	264	160	59	36	19	12	5	1	1	1

14,967 rolls is a relatively short test considering the Crap table on which these rolls occurred is operated 24 hours a day, 365 days a year. This sample leans toward Don't Pass. The next 24 hours may favor Pass Line.

72 HOURS AT THE CRAPS TABLE

- Roll by Roll -

6 10 3 2 7	O
6 7	O
3 − 7 − 10 10 − 12 − 6 4 7	CXXBO
2 − 4 3 8 8 7	2O
3 − 9 3 10 7	CO
8 6 9 4 9 7	O
9 10 6 10 8 8 2 6 5 7	O
6 6 − 5 8 8 12 6 8 7	XO
8 8 − 7 − 9 10 7	XXO
4 8 4 − 4 3 4 − 11 − 2 − 5 11 7	XXX2O
6 6 − 8 7	XO
7 − 6 10 4 7	XO
8 10 11 5 2 8 − 4 12 6 6 6 6 7	XO
2 − 7 − 4 5 7	2XO
7 − 12 − 9 8 5 9 − 8 6 7	XBXO
8 5 8 − 10 8 6 3 6 8 8 8 8 9 3 7	XO
8 7	O
6 9 6 − 6 9 10 10 8 11 10 5 6 − 5 3 4 8 7	XXO
6 4 11 6 − 3 − 6 5 5 9 12 7	XCO
9 7	O
8 6 10 11 5 5 9 5 9 4 8 − 3 − 8 5 7	XCO
4 10 8 6 8 5 5 3 10 5 7	O
8 8 − 6 6 − 10 8 5 10 − 5 6 11 2 11 8 4 9	XXX
12 10 5 − 6 5 9 8 5 5 7	XO
9 6 7	O
6 7	O
2 − 9 7	2O
8 4 4 8 − 7 − 7 − 5 7	XXXO
9 7	O
10 7	O
3 − 6 10 7	CO
10 8 7	O
7 − 11 − 9 7	XXO
9 9 − 7 − 7 − 5 9 7	XXXO

12 − 4 10 6 8 9 9 2 4 − 8 7	BXO
9 6 9 − 12 − 9 9 − 7 − 7 − 8 10 7	XBXXXO
5 10 5 − 7 − 3 − 9 6 12 9 − 11 − 9 12 5 8 9 −	XXCXXX
7 − 5 7	XO
7 − 3 − 8 8 − 8 6 7	XCXO
9 9 − 6 8 7	XO
8 6 11 10 3 7	O
8 9 8 − 4 5 6 6 7	XO
9 3 4 11 5 7	O
5 11 5 − 6 3 9 5 3 8 8 10 4 4 4 4 4 5 8 11	X
11 10 10 5 4 12 8 4 7	O
10 8 3 11 6 3 7	O
9 6 3 6 11 4 9 − 9 7	XO
7 − 11 − 3 − 3 − 10 7	XX CCO
5 10 10 9 12 7	O
3 − 7 − 5 7	CXO
6 10 9 5 9 6 − 11 − 6 8 4 5 7	XXO
9 4 8 5 5 9 − 5 7	XO
10 9 9 9 7	O
6 7	O
8 7	O
5 7	O
7 − 8 8 − 8 8 − 6 7	XXXO
7 − 7 − 12 − 8 6 8 − 5 7	XXBXO
4 7	O
6 6 − 4 7	XO
4 4 − 6 10 6 − 5 7	XXO
11 − 4 9 3 5 3 7	XO
11 − 4 7	XO
6 8 8 6 − 5 2 6 3 8 12 3 7	XO
6 9 6 − 9 8 12 9 − 7 − 9 8 7	XXXO
4 5 5 10 6 2 10 9 11 3 9 12 7	O
6 11 3 10 5 4 5 12 7	O
6 7	O

3 – 4 12 9 7	CO
7 – 4 6 11 7	XO
5 8 7	O
12 – 8 11 6 8 – 8 6 7	BXO
6 6 – 5 7	XO
5 6 11 11 3 8 10 10 6 10 9 6 6 7	O
11 – 6 7	XO
6 2 8 7	O
7 – 7 – 5 7	XXO
8 3 8 – 5 10 5 – 5 11 9 5 – 2 – 6 3 3 7	XXX2O
8 8 – 6 10 7	XO
8 5 7	O
11 – 11 – 6 9 12 10 6 – 7 – 5 8 6 11 4 7	XXXXO
8 7	O
4 7	O
6 3 6 – 8 5 9 9 10 8 – 11 – 4 8 3 12 5 9 5 6	XX
11 9 7	XO
5 6 8 4 9 6 8 8 7	O
5 7	O
8 6 7	O
4 7	O
7 – 4 11 7	XO
2 – 6 5 6 – 11 – 6 10 10 10 7	2 XXO
8 6 3 9 8 – 7 – 2 – 9 6 7	XX2O
8 9 6 10 11 10 8 – 7 – 8 7	XXO
7 – 6 9 6 – 2 – 2 – 7 – 7 – 6 10 8 6 –	XX22XXX
7 – 7 – 7 – 9 5 9 – 6 7	XXXXO
9 12 5 6 7	O
10 7	O
9 9 – 7 – 4 8 11 5 4 – 10 9 8 10 – 10 4 8	XXXX
6 4 8 9 8 4 6 5 11 6 4 8 9 10 – 8 6 10	XXXX
5 5 5 10 2 6 8 – 8 4 12 8 – 7 – 8 9 4 8 –	XXO
7 – 8 9 6 10 7	

7 – 12 – 12 – 5 6 11 5 – 7 – 5 6 2 5 – 12 –	XBBXXXB
11 – 5 4 6 10 8 7	XO
8 8 – 9 8 6 7	XO
5 4 8 4 9 8 4 9 6 3 5 – 8 5 4 3 4 12 9 9 5 7	XO
2 – 7 – 10 7	2XO
7 – 8 11 7	XO
9 6 8 9 – 7 – 6 6 – 10 11 7	XXXO
10 7	O
6 5 6 – 11 – 8 6 9 9 11 8 – 8 6 5 9 7	XXXO
10 6 9 11 5 9 5 7	O
5 10 3 3 7	O
12 – 10 8 7	BO
5 9 8 2 6 4 6 9 7	O
8 11 3 9 9 7	O
8 7	O
9 8 8 5 6 8 6 12 5 4 5 7	O
7 – 7 – 4 5 4 – 5 12 9 4 10 12 12 11 4 4 6	XXX
10 8 2 9 8 7	O
2 – 10 5 7	2O
10 11 7	O
5 5 – 6 6 – 7 – 8 10 8 – 6 9 9 11 9 2 3 8 6 –	XXXXX
5 11 8 12 9 7	O
5 3 9 6 4 12 6 5 – 9 7	XO
10 8 8 8 11 8 12 10 – 9 8 5 6 6 11 11 9 –	XX
9 8 3 7	O
6 7	O
8 12 7	O
8 2 5 4 8 – 8 8 – 10 11 8 8 9 12 9 3 5 3 6 5 7	XXO
5 3 9 8 6 11 6 10 10 8 7	O
7 – 7 – 9 11 11 3 7	XXO
9 9 – 10 2 7	XO
6 7	O
8 7	O
7 – 2 – 2 – 4 5 7	X22O
10 12 8 5 9 5 10 – 4 11 5 7	XO
7 – 7 – 8 4 5 7	XXO
7 – 8 8 – 5 7	XXO

6 6 − 7 − 6 4 5 6 − 11 − 6 6 − 4 9 9 6 9 10 7	XXXXXO
4 4 − 2 − 9 4 9 − 4 6 7	X2XO
11 − 6 3 10 9 7	XO
3 − 7 − 8 5 4 7	CXO
10 8 9 8 8 2 4 5 6 7	O
9 6 7	O
7 − 6 2 6 − 2 − 11 − 6 8 5 3 12 5 7	XX2XO
9 7	O
6 10 7	O
9 10 4 11 10 6 2 4 12 8 5 11 7	O
9 7	O
6 7	O
7 − 4 2 7	XO
6 6 − 8 11 6 5 6 6 9 8 − 9 10 3 4 8 4 3 7	XXO
4 10 5 5 8 7	O
6 7	O
9 5 5 4 7	O
4 9 7	O
8 8 − 3 − 5 3 5 − 11 − 6 9 8 7	XCXXO
6 7	O
5 6 7	O
4 7	O
10 11 8 7	O
3 − 7 − 6 7	CXO
4 7	O
6 3 3 5 7	O
9 10 9 − 3 − 8 4 6 6 3 9 4 8 − 10 11 5 6 8 7	XCXO
3 − 12 − 12 − 6 4 8 11 6 − 8 8 − 7 − 12 − 4 4 − 5 7	CBBXXXB XO
8 10 8 − 3 − 5 9 9 4 8 7	XCO
8 3 7	O
6 6 − 9 7	XO
12 − 6 11 8 7	BO
8 7	O
2 − 8 10 4 8 − 6 9 9 10 9 10 7	2XO

10 8 3 4 6 5 6 4 6 5 7	O
4 7	O
10 7	O
5 7	O
8 8 − 6 4 8 7	XO
7 − 10 9 4 6 9 10 − 7 − 6 5 8 7	XXXO
6 7	O
8 5 2 9 8 − 5 2 7	XO
7 − 9 7	XO
3 − 5 9 5 − 8 7	CXO
5 11 7	O
7 − 3 − 7 − 5 3 3 7	XCXO
2 − 7 − 12 − 10 6 4 10 − 12 − 9 8 8 3 4 11 6 7	2XBXBO
6 10 7	O
7 − 9 6 7	XO
10 5 7	O
4 4 − 10 4 9 6 8 2 12 8 4 8 10 − 5 7	XXO
7 − 6 9 9 5 7	XO
9 7	O
11 − 3 − 6 7	XCO
10 4 4 6 6 7	O
11 − 7 − 7 − 4 6 7	XXXO
10 8 9 7	O
4 8 5 8 6 4 − 3 − 5 5 − 8 9 3 5 4 7	XCXO
3 − 4 7	CO
9 8 7	O
9 8 9 − 3 − 6 11 7	XCO
11 − 7 − 9 4 7	XXO
7 − 5 5 − 8 11 10 6 7	XXO
8 7	O
4 5 8 10 6 7	O
5 10 5 − 8 7	XO
9 8 7	O
9 6 9 − 10 3 10 − 5 8 6 5 − 7 − 10 7	XXXXO
7 − 6 6 − 5 6 3 5 − 8 8 − 7 − 5 4 6 11 7	XXXXXO

▫▫▫▫▫°▫°°°°▫▫°▫°▫▫°▫▫°▫°▫°▫▫■▫■▫▫°▫▫°°°▫▫°▫°▫▫▫°▫▫°°°▫▫°▫°▫▫▫▫°▫▫°°▫°▫°▫▫▫°▫▫°°°°▫°▫°°°°°▫

4 9 8 10 5 5 10 7	O
5 7	O
10 3 8 5 9 8 9 9 2 8 9 7	O
5 6 8 10 3 8 7	O
8 7	O
7 – 11 – 6 7	XXO
7 – 9 7	XO
10 7	O
8 4 6 6 6 6 4 11 6 9 5 4 8 – 6 7	XO
12 – 8 8 – 11 – 3 – 8 6 6 8 – 8 5 4 6 6 6 9 3 7	BXXCXO
9 10 6 9 – 9 8 5 7	XO
3 – 5 5 – 7 – 6 7	CXXO
7 – 7 – 9 11 9 – 8 8 – 2 – 5 5 – 10 2 9 6 6	XXXX2X
11 11 4 12 9 8 11 7	O
3 – 7 – 2 – 11 – 9 6 4 7	CX2XO
5 4 5 – 3 – 6 3 11 5 9 3 7	XCO
5 5 – 8 5 10 4 2 5 11 7	XO
3 – 7 – 6 4 6 – 8 5 3 3 6 8 – 6 4 2 6 –	CXXXX
8 6 5 12 12 8 – 8 9 10 8 – 6 4 7	XXO
8 12 4 7	O
8 9 9 9 5 6 9 7	O
8 6 5 8 – 6 9 9 10 7	XO
7 – 6 12 2 8 12 7	XO
9 7	O
7 – 8 8 – 5 4 7	XXO
9 7	O
9 5 3 6 7	O
6 6 – 5 9 10 7	XO
8 6 8 – 6 4 3 10 12 7	XO
9 10 12 6 7	O
5 7	O
7 – 8 7	XO
12 – 9 11 8 3 6 10 10 6 9 – 8 10 5 10 7	BXO
7 – 9 9 – 6 7	XXO
10 7	O
7 – 9 10 7	XO

12 – 5 11 3 9 10 3 7	BO
8 9 9 9 10 7	O
7 – 9 10 5 7	XO
5 11 10 10 4 6 9 2 6 4 4 10 2 11 8 6 5 –	X
6 4 9 10 6 – 3 – 9 7	XCO
9 10 6 4 5 5 8 2 5 6 8 10 11 7	O
10 11 5 9 3 6 5 6 6 4 7	O
6 3 11 8 6 – 9 9 – 11 – 7 – 6 7	XXXXO
9 7	O
7 – 4 7	XO
5 6 6 8 5 – 7 – 11 – 6 8 6 – 5 7	XXXXO
12 – 5 4 5 – 6 7	BXO
8 10 5 12 6 11 6 9 5 7	O
7 – 9 5 2 8 4 7	XO
7 – 10 5 8 9 12 9 6 3 8 11 7	XO
4 8 8 7	O
8 6 5 6 7	O
4 12 4 – 10 4 5 12 11 6 6 12 2 7	XO
7 – 11 – 5 10 7	XXO
7 – 5 9 8 7	XO
3 – 9 7	CO
5 10 4 5 – 6 12 7	XO
10 4 11 6 5 5 10 – 10 7	XO
6 11 9 9 7	O
3 – 7 – 5 6 6 6 5 – 7 – 2 – 6 12 7	CXXX2O
7 – 6 10 4 8 10 3 6 – 3 – 3 – 4 10 7	XXCCO
10 10 – 5 6 4 3 5 – 8 10 9 5 8 – 5 9 6 8 8 9 4 6	XXX
9 9 10 5 – 9 11 5 9 – 2 – 9 9 – 4 7	XX2XO
5 7	O
6 9 8 9 9 7	O
7 – 8 7	XO
12 – 4 8 7	BO
4 4 – 7 – 10 8 3 7	XXO
6 11 11 7	O
8 8 – 12 – 8 5 7	XBO

6 7	O
11 − 4 5 5 11 2 9 7	XO
11 − 4 7	XO
7 − 10 5 6 11 6 8 3 8 8 4 2 7	XO
6 3 9 3 6 − 4 6 9 8 10 4 − 5 8 6 6 6 10 9 8 8 4 7	XXO
7 − 4 8 5 10 9 9 4 − 12 − 5 7	XXBO
8 9 6 10 6 10 10 5 7	O
3 − 7 − 5 6 9 8 11 9 7	CXO
8 8 − 10 6 8 4 2 6 9 7	XO
7 − 6 3 3 6 − 5 7	XXO
11 − 11 − 10 2 4 3 11 6 5 5 10 − 10 8 6 11	XX
4 6 4 7	XO
6 10 6 − 3 − 3 − 12 − 5 5 − 5 8 5 − 6 7	XCCBXXO
10 4 10 − 11 − 9 8 4 10 5 3 3 6 5 7	XXO
5 7	O
5 12 7	O
8 4 7	O
5 6 7	O
9 8 9 − 6 4 2 5 8 12 8 9 6 − 4 6 10 7	XXO
7 − 6 8 9 6 − 9 6 7	XXO
8 6 8 − 9 7	XO
12 − 8 10 7	BO
9 7	O
10 6 11 10 − 11 − 5 7	XXO
4 7	O
6 8 4 6 − 10 8 11 9 8 4 3 5 10 − 5 7	XXO
4 5 10 5 11 3 4 − 10 4 9 5 5 7	XO
7 − 6 6 − 3 − 7 − 8 4 8 − 5 7	XXCXXO
9 10 6 4 8 3 10 7	O
5 3 8 3 10 4 3 7	O
8 7	O
3 − 10 9 7	CO
8 9 7	O

7 – 12 – 9 10 6 8 4 3 3 9 – 3 – 8 10 8 –	XBXCX
11 – 7 – 8 5 8 – 5 3 8 5 – 6 2 6 – 5 7	XXXXXO
8 9 9 5 2 11 7	O
3 – 11 – 9 9 – 6 5 11 5 12 8 3 3 7	CXXO
3 – 6 5 5 7	CO
6 7	O
3 – 7 – 9 5 5 3 7	CXO
9 10 5 10 7	O
2 – 8 7	2O
7 – 8 9 10 7	XO
10 11 12 10 – 5 6 7	XO
11 – 4 10 11 7	XO
9 4 6 9 – 7 – 6 6 – 8 6 6 9 9 9 6 7	XXXO
3 – 12 – 11 – 6 5 5 11 6 – 7 – 3 – 3 – 2 –	CBXXX
9 4 7	CC2O
7 – 6 9 8 6 – 8 6 6 9 4 3 7	XXO
7 – 3 – 11 – 8 11 7	XCXO
7 – 7 – 4 8 10 8 3 8 7	XXO
6 7	O
3 – 5 11 5 – 4 3 5 5 10 5 11 9 9 8 6 12 9	CX
5 9 10 8 7	O
9 6 8 10 5 9 – 12 – 5 8 7	XBO
4 6 10 11 6 5 8 3 5 7	O
4 6 11 7	O
12 – 7 – 8 7	BXO
3 – 5 6 6 4 7	CO
11 – 8 7	XO
8 8 – 9 5 11 7	XO
7 – 9 10 7	XO
7 – 8 6 9 7	XO
5 9 2 10 8 2 5 – 4 7	XO
9 5 2 5 12 8 6 5 8 10 8 8 8 6 4 8 12 8 4 7	O
2 – 7 – 5 11 7	2 XO

```
11 – 8 4 8 – 9 10 3 7                                    XXO
11 – 6 9 9 10 5 10 6 – 7 – 9 8 8 9 – 7 – 8 8 –          XXXXX
  8 8 – 11 – 11 – 11 – 9 8 4 6 8 3 9 – 10 9 8 9 5        XXXXX
  9 6 8 8 12 6 8 10 – 10 8 11 5 10 – 8 10 10 7           XXXO
6 10 6 – 4 7                                             XO
12 – 11 – 11 – 9 4 6 10 7                                BXXO
9 11 5 3 7                                               O
7 – 7 – 10 5 7                                           XXO
6 8 3 7                                                  O
8 9 6 8 – 3 – 8 4 9 6 10 7                               XCO
10 11 7                                                  O
7 – 5 6 7                                                XO
2 – 5 7                                                  2O
7 – 5 4 7                                                XO
7 – 5 8 11 4 7                                           XO
2 – 2 – 7 – 5 6 6 8 7                                    22XO
4 8 6 8 7                                                O
7 – 7 – 5 5 – 10 9 8 3 10 – 5 5 – 9 9 – 5 5 –           XXXXX
  11 – 10 8 6 11 5 11 7                                  XXXO
11 – 5 8 11 8 8 9 11 6 8 10 6 7                          XO
7 – 9 7                                                  XO
4 6 7                                                    O
11 – 6 12 11 10 5 5 7                                    XO
6 8 9 7                                                  O
2 – 6 3 6 – 4 5 4 – 7 – 5 6 6 6 6 11 6 5 –              2XXXX
  8 9 6 4 5 10 4 8 – 5 6 10 5 – 8 7                      XXO
7 – 5 7                                                  XO
5 6 5 – 7 – 12 – 5 10 3 11 7                             XXBO
3 – 7 – 4 10 10 6 5 4 – 4 7                              CXXO
```

8 6 9 7	O
4 4 — 5 11 6 10 7	XO
6 6 — 7 — 10 11 9 6 7	XXO
8 8 — 5 **10** 5 — 6 6 — 7 — 9 11 7	XXXXO
12 — 8 7	BO
6 4 5 8 6 — 5 6 6 4 4 10 5 — 9 7	XXO
8 4 7	O
7 — 7 — **6** 10 10 9 7	XXO
5 6 8 **10 10** 8 8 5 — 7 — 8 5 9 8 — 12 — 7 —	XXXBX
6 9 12 5 4 11 5 **6** — 6 6 — 5 5 — 5 7	XXXO
11 — **10** 4 8 5 6 8 8 8 6 7	XO
4 5 7	O
2 — 11 — 10 5 4 6 3 7	2XO
8 9 11 8 — 9 5 11 3 8 9 — 9 3 6 11 6 8 10 7	XXO
5 5 — 9 7	XO
3 — 6 **10** 7	CO
9 9 — 2 — 12 — 8 6 **10** 5 7	X2BO
9 8 8 4 3 5 9 — 10 **10** — 5 5 — 12 — 9 4 7	XXXBO
3 — 8 8 — 6 7	CXO
3 — 9 5 7	CO
9 7	O
8 2 6 6 9 3 9 6 7	O
7 — 8 4 6 4 7	XO
6 9 6 — 11 — 3 — 12 — 5 10 4 5 — 7 — 4 7	XXCBXXO
10 5 7	O
9 11 7	O
4 3 7	O
6 10 10 5 10 7	O
10 7	O
6 9 10 9 6 — 8 7	XO
9 4 10 4 6 4 7	O
4 7	O
7 — 4 11 12 6 5 8 6 11 11 8 **10** 3 9 2 10 7	XO

6 9 6 − 3 − 8 7	XCO
5 7	O
8 9 7	O
5 9 9 4 6 6 8 5 − 8 5 8 − 12 − 3 − 4 5 5 7	XXBCO
6 8 9 7	O
10 7	O

6 3 8 4 8 11 6 − 2 − 6 4 9 9 9 10 5 12 6 −
    3 − 9 7
	X2X
	  CO

6 6 − 3 − 5 9 6 9 8 9 4 11 6 7	XCO
8 4 10 6 6 3 11 4 8 − 12 − 10 9 10 − 10 4 7	XBXO
8 8 − 4 4 − 9 4 9 − 11 − 11 − 6 12 9 9 **10** 11 9 7	XXXXXO
7 − 11 − 9 6 11 3 11 7	XXO
6 4 6 − 11 − 7 − 7 − 9 7	XXXXO
8 7	O
7 − 4 3 7	XO
8 12 8 − 4 5 5 7	XO
7 − 10 3 5 6 4 10 − 9 7	XXO
4 **10** 5 7	O
12 − 3 − 6 11 **10** 6 − 9 6 7	BCXO
11 − 6 6 − 8 10 9 3 3 7	XXO
12 − 8 7	BO
9 8 10 10 11 7	O
2 − 10 7	2O

3 − 8 11 9 4 10 6 5 3 5 8 − 8 6 9 9 8 − 8 8 −
    3 − 6 7
	CXXX
	  CO

9 10 7	O
12 − 4 6 7	BO
5 7	O
7 − 8 8 − 3 − 8 8 − 6 7	XXCXO
4 6 7	O
7 − 8 7	XO
10 12 10 − 10 6 9 9 7	XO

3 − 6 3 6 − 5 7	CXO
6 10 7	O
7 − 6 10 8 5 7	XO
9 7	O
7 − 12 − 3 − 10 3 8 7	XBCO
11 − 7 − 7 − 8 8 − 6 5 10 7	XXXXO
12 − 2 − 6 7	B2O
8 9 6 10 7	O
7 − 6 4 8 5 11 9 11 9 5 7	XO
6 6 − 6 5 7	XO
8 10 4 4 11 3 7	O
8 7	O
3 − 10 7	CO
6 6 − 9 7	XO
6 9 6 − 6 7	XO
8 9 8 − 8 7	XO
6 9 9 5 8 10 9 3 8 9 7	O
11 − 8 4 8 − 4 6 4 − 3 − 5 7	XXXCO
10 9 9 5 4 7	O
6 11 7	O
2 − 7 − 3 − 12 − 7 − 8 7	2XCBXO
4 11 5 7	O
7 − 7 − 4 6 12 3 8 4 − 6 7	XXXO
4 8 4 − 10 6 8 2 8 7	XO
7 − 5 6 4 2 8 11 8 7	XO
7 − 8 7	XO
3 − 4 6 12 11 7	CO
5 2 4 4 8 4 9 4 9 8 5 − 5 4 8 7	XO
6 9 8 8 6 − 5 9 6 6 12 7	XO
5 7	O
6 5 5 7	O
6 8 9 6 − 7 − 6 7	XXO
7 − 9 11 11 7	XO
5 6 11 7	O
6 9 5 6 − 4 8 7	XO
3 − 11 − 11 − 4 5 11 11 4 − 5 4 9 8 7	CXXXO

5 5 − 5 8 11 7	XO
11 − 4 7	XO
8 5 7	O
12 − 2 − 6 5 2 2 9 7	B2O
4 4 − 9 8 8 3 11 10 7	XO
5 4 10 6 7	O
10 3 5 6 4 5 11 8 12 2 8 8 6 7	O
5 6 5 − 9 9 − 10 8 6 9 11 9 8 2 12 12 3 3 4 8 9 7	XXO
8 6 11 11 10 6 5 8 − 6 8 7	XO
10 4 8 9 8 3 5 8 6 8 5 9 6 7	O
·8 6 8 − 6 8 5 4 6 − 9 11 6 5 9 − 5 6 5 − 6 11	XXXX
3 4 9 5 9 4 8 10 5 9 2 10 6 − 7 − 9 12 10 9 −	XXX
10 8 8 6 7	O
7 − 8 3 5 5 10 11 6 5 8 − 3 − 8 3 2 8 −	XXCX
5 11 10 9 7	O
5 4 8 6 3 6 8 9 7	O
6 6 − 7 − 4 8 3 5 5 6 7	XXO
10 5 8 6 6 7	O
7 − 9 5 6 9 − 4 7	XXO
11 − 9 7	XO
7 − 3 − 8 7	XCO
8 8 − 6 10 5 6 − 9 7	XXO
8 8 − 4 8 5 2 5 7	XO
11 − 4 9 8 10 5 6 7	XO
2 − 6 2 5 5 7	2O
10 11 10 − 6 10 9 11 4 11 5 7	XO
7 − 2 − 10 5 10 − 5 4 7	X2XO
6 9 9 9 4 7	O
9 3 6 8 7	O
3 − 9 4 9 − 5 7	CXO
8 9 5 3 8 − 6 4 10 10 5 11 8 5 3 5 5 9 6 −	XX
8 9 7	O
5 7	O
10 6 9 7	O
6 10 7	O
11 − 9 7	XO
7 − 5 6 9 6 7	XO
8 10 8 − 2 − 9 3 8 10 9 − 5 4 11 3 7	X2XO

7 − 8 2 6 9 8 − 9 6 8 9 − 9 10 9 − 10 11 9 6 7	XXXXO
3 − 7 − 6 7	CXO
4 5 5 5 7	O
12 − 8 8 − 4 5 8 7	BXO
12 − 5 6 4 11 4 7	BO
10 5 5 5 5 4 7	O
6 4 9 6 − 9 7	XO
11 − 8 9 11 4 7	XO
8 4 5 4 6 5 6 9 6 6 5 10 6 3 4 4 9 11 10 5 5	
11 5 9 10 10 2 6 5 7	O
7 − 6 4 4 12 6 − 8 6 7	XXO
9 8 6 5 7	O
9 8 7	O
8 9 8 − 6 11 11 8 6 − 6 5 11 5 12 5 8 7	XXO
5 8 8 11 8 2 7	O
2 − 10 7	2O
6 6 − 10 7	XO
8 5 10 10 9 7	O
5 12 8 6 7	O
4 9 7	O
9 6 8 7	O
8 4 6 8 − 8 4 10 9 6 10 7	XO
8 9 6 8 − 3 − 8 6 3 8 − 5 7	XCXO
6 3 9 6 − 6 10 2 9 10 8 6 − 5 10 12 3 3 9 7	XXO
6 9 4 10 5 7	O
5 5 − 2 − 5 3 9 4 8 7	X2O
2 − 10 8 6 4 6 8 6 9 12 3 7	2O
8 6 2 9 3 4 7	O
8 7	O
8 9 9 6 5 9 10 3 6 6 8 − 2 − 4 7	X2O
6 3 7	O
7 − 7 − 10 4 2 7	XXO
7 − 4 11 8 6 4 − 8 8 − 5 5 − 9 7	XXXXO
2 − 8 7	2O
7 − 11 − 8 8 − 7 − 3 − 5 3 7	XXXXCO
7 − 6 11 8 10 10 6 − 3 − 5 4 12 9 12 10 10 7	XXCO

3 – 9 9 – 12 – 12 – 6 8 4 7	CXBBO
11 – 8 12 10 7	XO
7 – 4 8 8 7	XO
6 4 12 5 5 3 8 12 9 6 – 6 9 8 7	XO
9 4 4 6 7	O
6 6 – 6 8 7	XO
7 – 5 6 7	XO
5 10 5 – 3 – 10 5 9 6 5 9 8 5 9 9 9 10 – 4 7	XCXO
9 10 11 3 8 10 8 5 6 8 9 – 7 – 4 4 – 4 7	XXXO
6 8 9 8 10 9 10 3 6 – 10 7	XO
9 8 11 8 10 6 6 9 – 3 – 7 – 10 5 6 9 6 10 –	XCXX
8 8 – 8 10 12 2 12 4 7	XO
11 – 10 3 11 8 12 10 – 5 8 8 5 – 6 3 9 5 4 7	XXXO
11 – 5 10 3 8 8 4 12 5 – 5 8 5 – 8 7	XXXO
10 10 – 8 7	XO
3 – 4 9 7	CO
8 6 7	O
7 – 12 – 8 11 6 8 – 12 – 11 – 3 – 8 8 – 11 –	XBXBXC
3 – 2 – 5 7	XXC2O
5 10 6 6 7	O
5 8 4 7	O
2 – 4 7	2O
12 – 8 4 3 3 8 – 3 – 3 – 7 – 6 7	BXCCXO
9 7	O
4 6 6 8 10 7	O
7 – 5 10 8 6 7	XO
11 – 2 – 9 8 7	X2O
8 7	O
8 5 5 4 11 6 7	O
4 7	O
8 10 4 7	O
4 3 6 7	O
2 – 4 6 9 8 10 9 12 7	2O

8 7	O
8 8 − 7 − 10 10 − 4 4 − 6 6 − 5 7	XXXXXO
6 5 11 3 4 4 8 5 7	O
7 − 7 − 9 2 10 7	XXO
7 − 5 11 4 3 7	XO
6 8 11 5 10 6 − 7 − 7 − 11 − 10 3 9 3 5 3 8	XXXX
9 6 3 11 4 4 9 6 7	O
7 − 5 5 − 7 − 9 4 2 8 7	XXXO
9 7	O
7 − 10 9 11 8 8 7	XO
2 − 6 8 6 − 8 11 5 7	2XO
5 8 10 9 11 9 7	O
3 − 9 11 7	CO
10 8 6 9 10 − 3 − 11 − 9 12 3 11 12 5 6 7	XCXO
7 − 5 5 − 10 12 9 7	XXO
11 − 6 6 − 4 8 11 6 9 5 6 5 8 6 6 7	XXO
7 − 6 11 6 − 7 − 5 7	XXXO
6 5 4 9 5 11 11 9 12 7	O
7 − 10 3 10 − 5 7	XXO
8 4 8 − 8 6 10 7	XO
7 − 4 5 8 8 11 8 10 11 6 11 6 8 6 5 3 10 8 5 7	XO
9 7	O
9 7	O
7 − 8 9 7	XO
2 − 5 8 8 7	2O
7 − 6 4 4 8 4 4 7	XO
5 4 7	O
4 9 4 − 10 6 4 4 10 − 4 11 6 6 4 − 9 5 11 9 −	XXXX
8 6 2 4 9 4 8 − 9 4 5 8 7	XO
8 7	O
5 6 5 − 8 6 7	XO
6 6 − 3 − 4 5 3 8 6 5 7	XCO
10 11 4 8 6 4 3 8 8 10 − 5 6 12 9 6 8 3 9 9 9 7	XO
9 6 10 4 6 9 − 7 − 8 8 − 8 12 7	XXXO

8 9 6 9 7	O
10 6 5 4 8 10 − 4 3 10 6 11 10 8 5 10 8 4 − 7 −	XXX
11 − 8 5 7	XO
6 7	O
5 10 6 4 7	O
10 4 8 7	O
9 9 − 9 7	XO
4 8 11 4 − 6 11 6 − 6 5 3 5 5 4 10 10 7	XXO
12 − 7 − 9 7	BXO
8 9 11 9 12 4 6 3 11 7	O
12 − 7 − 4 5 2 5 6 6 4 − 9 7	BXXO
5 10 6 8 6 12 7	O
5 8 7	O
9 8 11 9 − 5 4 5 − 3 − 6 10 8 5 9 4 10 6 − 10 7	XXCXO
7 − 7 − 3 − 6 10 8 12 7	XXCO
7 − 7 − 9 7	XXO
8 5 8 − 7 − 5 11 6 6 3 6 10 5 − 6 7	XXXO
10 3 9 3 8 10 − 11 − 6 7	XXO
5 11 7	O
6 7	O
11 − 8 12 11 3 9 6 8 − 6 10 7	XXO
10 4 4 9 10 − 8 3 4 10 9 2 6 8 − 6 4 9 7	XXO
9 8 7	O
8 11 9 5 6 6 6 6 9 7	O
10 8 7	O
8 10 8 − 6 4 5 5 10 11 7	XO
5 9 4 4 11 4 8 5 − 6 8 5 9 7	XO
7 − 11 − 7 − 9 8 5 6 4 8 6 3 10 7	XXXO
10 7	O
5 6 11 9 8 8 7	O
7 − 10 5 11 9 8 9 4 10 − 7 − 11 − 8 6 7	XXXXO
8 8 − 10 6 11 8 3 10 − 7 − 3 − 7 − 9 8 8 7	XXXCXO
9 5 10 8 7	O
5 4 7	O
8 12 4 7	O
5 7	O
8 4 7	O

4 4 − 6 8 7	XO
7 − 5 5 − 7 − **10** 8 10 − 12 − 4 4 − 6 10 5 8 8	XXXXBX
12 5 6 − 7 − 9 8 4 8 8 12 9 − 7 − 6 11 3 5	XXXX
4 11 5 9 5 12 5 10 4 7	O
5 9 3 7	O
12 − **6** 6 − 9 7	BXO
7 − 7 − 8 8 − 4 6 7	XXXO
7 − 11 − 6 3 6 − 7 − 6 10 12 2 7	XXXXO
7 − 3 − 7 − 7 − 9 9 − 6 11 5 5 7	XCXXXO
10 2 7	O
10 4 4 7	O
5 3 9 3 6 10 5 − 7 − 5 12 7	XXO
9 7	O
5 8 12 5 − 4 4 − 9 8 4 6 5 10 5 6 **10** 11 5 6 6 9 −	XXX
8 6 7	O
3 − 5 5 − 4 3 11 3 4 − 7 − 7 − 5 7	CXXXO
6 2 8 9 9 4 11 4 4 3 6 − 3 − 7 − 3 − 3 − 4 11 7	XCXCCO
7 − 11 − 6 10 7	XXO
11 − 5 7	XO
7 − 6 7	XO
6 10 3 9 11 6 − 3 − **6** 6 − 3 − 3 − 6 7	XCXCCO
7 − 7 − 6 6 − 6 9 11 7	XXXO
9 4 6 8 6 4 5 7	O
10 9 **10** − 3 − 7 − 6 7	XCXO
6 2 7	O
9 5 7	O

11 – 3 – 2 – 7 – 8 6 8 – 8 10 3 6 **10** 5 7	XC2XXO
9 8 5 8 9 – 8 5 12 7	XO
7 – 6 4 9 8 9 9 4 8 9 5 5 **10** 6 – 3 – 7 – 9 11 7	XXCXO
7 – 8 4 7	XO
6 8 8 8 9 8 9 7	O
6 4 6 – 8 4 10 4 9 7	XO
6 4 3 9 6 – 8 8 – 6 7	XXO
10 4 8 6 9 3 7	O
6 12 9 2 9 2 4 5 6 – 7 – 9 5 7	XXO
7 – 6 7	XO
10 8 6 9 7	O
10 7	O
9 3 5 9 – 8 8 – 2 – 12 – 6 7	XX2BO
4 10 7	O
7 – 9 8 8 3 10 3 4 9 – 9 7	XXO
11 – 3 – 7 – 8 7	XCXO
4 5 10 7	O
3 – 7 – 8 7	CXO
3 – 7 – 7 – 7 – 8 6 6 3 8 – 5 5 – 7 – 7 – 4 3 8 3 5 2 7	CXXXXX XXO
10 8 6 7	O
7 – 11 – 6 12 11 10 5 2 3 4 7	XXO
3 – 6 6 – 8 10 7	CXO
7 – 5 7	XO
9 8 7	O
3 – 7 – 12 – 8 5 4 3 6 3 11 4 5 6 8 – 9 6 11 10 7	CXBX O
6 9 6 – 3 – 10 7	XCO
8 4 8 – 10 8 6 8 8 12 7	XO
2 – 4 6 8 9 7	2O
5 5 – 6 9 9 9 9 5 7	XO

6 3 6 − 7 − 6 6 − 9 6 5 10 3 9 − 6 7	XXXXO
7 − 6 8 6 − 7 − 7 − 10 4 4 6 12 9 8 11 11 6 7	XXXXO
10 10 − 10 4 2 11 9 7	XO
2 − 9 6 11 8 8 4 10 7	2O
8 6 8 − 6 6 − 7 − 8 6 7	XXXO
8 4 12 6 12 4 7	O
6 6 − 7 − 6 7	XXO
7 − 6 10 9 8 10 8 11 10 11 4 7	XO
3 − 9 9 − 7 − 8 4 3 8 − 7 − 6 5 7	CXXXXO
8 4 4 3 11 6 4 4 8 − 9 7	XO
6 6 − 3 − 4 9 7	XCO
11 − 7 − 5 4 8 5 − 12 − 10 6 10 − 7 −	XXXBXX
7 − 8 11 6 9 7	XO
6 5 8 2 6 − 5 7	XO
10 3 7	O
9 11 8 10 7	O
3 − 10 7	CO
4 4 − 8 8 − 4 7	XXO
4 2 8 7	O
10 7	O
12 − 8 7	BO
10 8 7	O
11 − 3 − 2 − 7 − 6 7	XC2XO
5 9 2 6 4 7	O
7 − 7 − 6 4 4 4 7	XXO
11 − 9 8 11 7	XO
9 7	O
10 4 6 7	O
4 8 10 3 8 6 11 10 11 7	O
8 6 8 − 11 − 7 − 6 7	XXXO
3 − 4 7	CO
3 − 5 9 10 7	CO

10 10 – 8 2 6 5 7	XO
5 9 6 5 – 11 – 8 11 4 8 – 10 4 2 10 – 7 –	XXXXX
10 10 – 9 7	XO
4 9 4 – 5 3 4 9 7	XO
6 10 8 6 – 10 5 7	XO
7 – 5 3 5 – 5 5 – 2 – 3 – 6 7	XXX2CO
5 9 9 12 4 8 9 10 2 5 – 4 5 8 8 8 10 8 12	XX
8 6 4 – 8 7	O
4 7	O
8 4 3 8 – 6 10 9 7	XO
4 12 6 8 8 10 4 – 4 8 8 6 7	XO
4 8 3 8 2 8 8 4 – 9 2 8 8 8 9 – 4 7	XXO
6 11 8 6 – 5 7	XO
12 – 6 6 – 4 10 10 3 8 11 8 7	BXO
7 – 4 8 8 8 7	XO
3 – 5 6 8 6 2 9 5 – 7 – 6 9 7	CXXO
5 9 7	O
6 5 9 9 7	O
8 2 9 5 9 3 8 – 5 3 6 8 7	XO
11 – 2 – 7 – 2 – 9 7	X2X2O
9 9 – 7 – 5 8 2 9 8 5 – 7 – 10 7	XXXXO
7 – 7 – 8 6 7	XXO
11 – 9 8 5 8 9 – 7 – 6 8 9 6 – 10 11 10 – 4 8 7	XXXXXO
10 9 5 10 – 6 9 10 3 8 8 7	XO
5 6 7	O
3 – 4 11 11 4 – 7 – 8 9 9 6 7	CXXO
10 12 8 5 2 7	O
2 – 6 8 8 10 7	2O
9 5 6 5 8 7	O
7 – 7 – 11 – 9 4 10 2 7	XXXO

9 6 9 – 8 **10 8** – 4 6 8 4 – 7 – 5 9 10 9 4	XXXX
4 6 9 9 3 8 8 9 12 6 7	O
7 – 7 – 11 – 8 8 – 11 – 9 6 7	XXXXXO
4 9 4 – 7 – 8 3 **10** 10 6 12 7	XXO
8 9 7	O
10 8 **10** – 6 10 3 9 7	XO
4 5 5 5 5 8 8 10 6 9 8 7	O
3 – 5 8 6 8 9 12 4 5 – 9 27	CXO
7 – 6 12 7	XO
8 6 11 9 10 6 9 4 8 – 6 7	XO
11 – 8 5 6 8 – 8 8 – 8 11 8 – 7 – 6 9 4 9 7	XXXXXO
11 – 7 – 8 5 7	XXO
7 – 4 5 **10** 8 9 6 3 6 3 6 3 8 5 3 7	XO
4 8 10 4 – 11 – 4 5 3 10 6 5 10 9 9 10 3 8	XX
9 5 6 4 – 12 – 5 3 9 7	XBO
6 8 7	O
7 – 10 5 6 6 5 5 7	XO
4 8 9 8 12 6 6 10 4 – 8 9 7	XO
4 8 5 8 9 12 7	O
6 5 4 6 – 3 – 6 8 3 5 5 6 – 6 9 6 – 4 8 10 2 7	XCXXO
11 – 10 3 7	XO
6 6 – 3 – 5 8 8 8 7	XCO
9 7	O
9 5 8 6 5 11 9 – 6 5 8 10 5 **10** 10 6 – 3 –	XXC
4 **10** 8 9 3 6 9 11 3 9 5 5 5 7	O
7 – 8 4 3 9 10 5 11 7	XO
12 – 10 5 12 6 **8** 5 8 9 10 – 9 8 7	BXO
3 – 6 3 7	CO
4 8 2 7	O
11 – 11 – 6 4 7	XXO
10 8 9 8 3 3 4 6 9 4 6 8 9 9 7	O
4 9 10 12 6 9 3 6 6 7	O
4 5 8 11 6 10 8 7	O
5 7	O

10 10 − 3 − 9 11 6 8 11 7	XCO
6 5 9 10 9 5 7	O
4 5 7	O
3 − 5 8 6 5 − 7 − 5 9 8 10 6 8 5 − 9 9 −	CXXXX
5 10 9 9 10 4 9 5 − 9 4 6 4 6 5 7	XO
9 8 10 3 10 **8** 12 9 − 8 **10** 5 6 8 −	XX
8 4 5 2 6 12 11 12 9 7	O
8 7	O
6 8 6 − 8 7	XO
11 − 10 **10** − 12 − 4 7	XXBO
9 9 − 6 7	XO
9 9 − 4 8 7	XO
4 10 6 10 10 8 8 4 − 10 3 6 7	XO
7 − 12 − 8 2 7	XBO
10 8 7	O
11 − 7 − 7 − 3 − 11 − 9 6 **6** 8 7	XXXCXO
10 9 4 7	O
8 4 9 4 6 6 9 6 9 7	O
9 4 8 4 3 6 8 6 9 − 7 − 7 − 9 10 10 3 8 11 10	XXX
10 8 5 5 5 6 4 12 6 7	O
7 − 5 8 6 **10** 10 8 5 − **10** 2 5 2 7	XXO
4 7	O
2 − 7 − 7 − 7 − 8 **8** − 2 − 6 7	2XXXX2O
6 7	O
8 8 − 6 9 6 − 9 6 3 7	XXO
6 6 − 5 8 7	XO
9 10 8 11 7	O
6 12 8 **10** 7	O
6 11 7	O
6 8 11 12 11 7	O
7 − 9 7	XO
8 8 − 11 − 4 6 11 3 8 8 9 7	XXO
6 9 6 − 4 11 2 6 5 4 − 12 − 8 **10** 6 5 8 −	XXBX
3 − 11 − 10 2 3 7	CXO
8 7	O

88 – 55 – 834598 – 7 – 89458 –	XXXXX
12 – 468987	BO
7 – 9589 – 957	XXO
867	O
10 483547	O
87	O
657	O
9 116 8 10 859 – 498 11 7	XO
44 – 464 – 107	XXO
103 **10** – 7 – 7 – 9 **10** 7	XXXO
47	O
5 10 5 – 11 – 4 10 5 2 8 6 12 3 3 12 4 –	XXX
6 11 7	O
7 – 7 – 11 – 63 11 3 11 86 – 11 – 10 12 5	XXXXX
999957	O
10 47	O
7 – 105 10 – 88 – 66 – 10 9 65 65 12 87	XXXXO
97	O
4937	O
8 658 – 3 – 8 11 5 10 5 7	XCO
7 – 11 – 547	XXO
7 – 957	XO
49687	O
49655687	O
687	O
12 – **10** 6 666 11 8 11 7	BO
97	O
8 12 **10** 6 7	O
105537	O
3 – 87	CO
96637	O
7 – 456267	XO
959 – 3 – 897	XCO
8 45 5 10 12 45 11 3 5 5 7	O
69 10 87	O
5 885 – 7 – **10** 85 69 64 65 687	XXO
7 – 87	XO

4 8 5 3 12 6 7	O
6 7	O
12 − 4 3 9 4 − 9 9 − 7 − 4 8 3 5 8 8 5 8	BXXX
11 6 9 7	O
8 10 5 8 − 9 7	XO
10 10 − 7 − 5 12 9 3 7	XXO
6 8 9 6 − 10 4 6 9 12 7	XO
4 4 − 7 − 9 5 6 4 9 − 7 − 3 − 6 6 − 7 −	XXXXCXX
6 11 9 7	O
10 6 7	O
4 4 − 2 − 8 9 4 5 6 6 6 5 2 9 10 9 4 5 7	X2O
9 10 10 7	O
9 11 12 8 6 11 8 10 8 10 6 9 − 6 5 8 7	XO
8 10 7	O
6 8 2 5 7	O
9 6 8 7	O
9 12 8 4 6 11 8 7	O
8 6 5 2 7	O
7 − 2 − 8 9 11 5 5 4 10 3 3 5 8 − 7 − 6 8 7	X2XXO
6 8 3 4 6 − 5 9 5 − 8 6 7	XXO
12 − 8 5 4 3 5 9 7	BO
6 6 − 6 9 6 − 6 10 4 7	XXO
6 6 − 11 − 10 12 8 5 6 3 9 8 7	XXO
3 − 11 − 10 7	CXO
8 11 4 12 5 6 7	O
5 3 5 − 10 7	XO
4 7	O
12 − 9 9 − 11 − 8 7	BXXO
10 6 10 − 6 9 6 − 11 − 5 7	XXXO
10 8 5 10 − 7 − 7 − 10 10 − 7 − 3 − 12 −	XXXXXCB
2 − 10 6 8 10 − 7 − 7 − 5 7	2XXXO
4 8 9 8 8 9 4 − 12 − 8 6 3 8 − 8 5 7	XBXO

7 − 7 − 7 − 9 4 4 5 5 9 − 6 8 11 4 9 8 8 7	XXXXO
4 7	O
7 − 5 4 7	XO
4 8 12 6 2 10 6 9 7	O
11 − 4 12 5 12 12 5 5 5 6 6 8 8 7	XO
7 − 6 6 − 8 3 7	XXO
2 − 6 7	2O
5 11 8 8 6 2 7	O
5 7	O
5 8 7	O
5 8 6 9 10 8 7	O
11 − 9 6 9 − 12 − 11 − 7 − 10 6 4 7	XXBXXO
7 − 6 9 8 5 6 − 9 7	XXO
8 2 9 7	O
11 − 8 7	XO
3 − 6 11 7	CO
10 6 8 8 3 10 − 7 − 5 7	XXO
8 5 4 3 7	O
3 − 7 − 3 − 4 6 5 11 10 8 8 4 − 5 11 10 7	CXCXO
8 8 − 7 − 7 − 8 9 5 6 6 6 8 − 3 − 8 6 7	XXXXCO
7 − 10 7	XO
9 2 7	O
7 − 9 6 7	XO
11 − 8 12 6 7	XO
7 − 7 − 3 − 3 − 6 6 − 11 − 6 4 7	XXCCXXO
3 − 10 11 3 7	CO
6 7	O
5 6 10 6 4 6 10 6 8 12 9 5 − 7 − 6 11 7	XXO
11 − 10 8 6 11 7	XO
5 7	O
9 6 9 − 4 7	XO
10 6 6 6 9 4 9 5 8 8 6 3 5 10 − 10 7	XO
5 11 10 9 7	O
6 5 7	O
9 7	O

7 – 3 – 6 7	XCO
4 9 11 7	O
9 12 8 7	O
7 – 7 – 5 8 8 6 6 5 – 4 7	XXXO
7 – 6 6 – 7 – 9 11 10 3 4 7	XXXO
10 8 6 7	O
11 – 10 6 6 12 7	XO
2 – 4 10 11 4 – 12 – 12 – 8 8 – 11 – 3 – 11 –	2XBBXXCX
7 – 4 8 10 9 7	XO
6 10 9 9 10 9 7	O
5 8 10 3 4 7	O
5 5 – 6 7	XO
5 5 – 7 – 3 – 12 – 10 5 10 – 5 8 6 9 8 5 –	XXCBXX
5 7	O
7 – 9 11 10 4 5 6 7	XO
7 – 6 8 2 6 – 3 – 5 2 10 7	XXCO
10 7	O
5 11 4 10 3 7	O
5 9 8 6 7	O
12 – 10 9 4 6 7	BO
5 3 10 3 10 9 6 6 5 – 11 – 10 11 9 6 7	XXO
9 8 4 6 6 8 4 3 12 7	O
9 5 7	O
10 10 – 8 8 – 9 10 6 9 – 12 – 5 12 7	XXXBO
7 – 7 – 7 – 9 6 5 8 8 9 – 10 8 4 8 6 4 6 4 3 7	XXXXO
2 – 6 7	2O
5 6 5 – 2 – 10 1 8 10 – 10 2 8 8 2 5 10 – 7 –	X2XXX
4 11 9 9 4 – 7 – 7 – 9 11 7	XXXO
3 – 5 7	CO
5 7	O
7 – 6 5 6 – 8 4 4 12 4 10 6 10 11 11 7	XXO

4 5 5 8 6 4 − 3 − 5 12 7	XCO
8 11 5 6 2 10 4 6 7	O
5 39 10 8 9 2 11 8 7	O
11 − 6 5 5 2 8 2 6 − 8 8 − 7 − 7 − 9 3 7	XXXXXO
9 2 8 12 9 − 6 6 − 11 − 8 8 − 3 − 8 10 10 8 −	XXXXCX
4 11 7	O
11 − 8 6 9 3 6 5 8 − 5 5 − 8 8 − 8 6 4 4 9 8 −	XXXXX
9 5 8 3 5 9 − 3 − 10 8 4 4 2 4 6 8 7	XCO
7 − 6 7	XO
5 3 8 9 10 10 8 7	O
3 − 3 − 7 − 5 8 6 5 − 6 6 − 9 10 7	CCXXXO
8 11 4 7	O
6 3 8 6 − 10 7	XO
12 − 6 8 7	BO
8 6 8 − 5 11 7	XO
5 7	O
8 8 − 7 − 7 − 5 7	XXXO
9 7	O
10 4 11 5 3 7	O
3 − 6 8 11 5 12 10 12 7	CO
5 8 5 − 7 − 8 8 − 8 6 3 9 8 − 9 7	XXXXO
6 2 7	O
9 7	O
9 7	O
7 − 5 10 4 7	XO
7 − 2 − 9 7	X2O
7 − 7 − 8 2 7	XXO
12 − 9 4 8 8 6 2 6 11 11 8 2 7	BO
7 − 5 7	XO
4 3 8 5 12 6 6 7	O
5 12 9 7	O
8 7	O
3 − 6 7	CO
8 3 5 5 11 6 5 4 4 11 6 7	O

10 10 − 6 10 6 − 6 9 6 − 5 8 5 − 7 −	XXXXX
3 − 9 5 5 8 5 117	CO
4 7	O
10 9 7	O
10 6 4 8 8 7	O
4 2 11 6 7	O
10 5 10 − 7 − 6 3 10 8 12 8 6 − 5 3 6 7	XXXO
8 7	O
11 − 7 − 11 − 7 − 8 9 6 8 − 8 9 **10** 11 4 12	XXXXX
9 9 4 5 6 5 3 7	O
4 4 − 5 6 10 7	XO
5 9 8 5 − 10 10 − 8 7	XXO
3 − 3 − 7 − 11 − 3 − 4 8 9 7	CCXXCO
9 8 7	O
10 3 6 **8** 5 8 6 **8** 2 12 10 − 4 11 6 9 3 9 5 4 − 9 7	XXO
9 8 5 5 5 11 7	O
4 10 11 2 9 6 7	O
10 8 12 7	O
4 7	O
7 − 8 12 7	XO
4 12 8 6 2 8 7	O
9 11 3 7	O
5 5 − 4 10 7	XO
5 22 10 10 5 − 8 7	XO
9 9 − 7 − 8 4 8 − 4 **10** 10 7	XXXO
9 8 6 6 9 − 3 − 11 − 4 8 5 12 2 7	XCXO
10 7	O
5 6 4 10 6 8 4 9 10 9 11 8 9 8 8 8 8 7	O
8 2 6 6 8 − 11 − **8** 5 12 9 3 4 7	XXO
8 5 6 6 8 − 4 7	XO
4 4 − 8 6 7	XO
6 2 7	O
7 − 4 6 4 − 2 − 8 5 10 8 − 3 − 9 7	XX2XCO
8 6 3 9 5 6 7	O
8 10 9 10 10 8 − 9 4 6 11 3 5 11 7	XO
8 7	O

```
6 3 4 8 8 4 4 4 6 — 8 12 8 — 5 8 12 5 —          XXX
   8 6 10 6 7                                      O
6 7                                                O
2 — 2 — 12 — 9 7                                   22BO
10 4 7                                             O
10 5 6 11 8 3 2 10 — 7 — 11 — 9 6 6 6 6 9 — 9 7    XXXXO
2 — 7 — 6 7                                        2XO
7 — 5 11 3 6 5 — 7 — 8 7                           XXXO
10 7                                               O
9 8 7                                              O
2 — 8 8 — 6 9 2 9 5 4 6 — 12 — 10 4 5 10 —         2XXBX
   7 — 11 — 10 6 7                                  XXO
10 8 9 8 10 — 10 7                                 XO
3 — 8 7                                            CO
6 9 4 7                                            O
8 8 — 5 8 8 5 — 6 5 5 9 7                          XXO
5 7                                                O
6 9 9 4 6 — 11 — 10 2 10 — 9 5 7                   XXXO
4 7                                                O
2 — 9 5 11 3 7                                     2O
6 9 6 — 6 7                                        XO
7 — 10 7                                           XO
2 — 3 — 9 6 8 11 7                                 2CO
12 — 10 6 5 8 10 — 4 8 7                           BXO
6 7                                                O
7 — 11 — 10 9 2 7                                  XXO
3 — 7 — 3 — 7 — 7 — 5 2 6 7                        CXCXXO
4 9 5 7                                            O
4 7                                                O
6 8 6 — 5 4 3 6 8 6 7                              XO
8 8 — 12 — 6 8 7                                   XBO
5 7                                                O
```

8 8 − 6 6 − 7 − 7 − 6 9 5 7	XXXXO
8 2 9 8 − 11 − 11 − 3 − 10 6 6 9 4 2 9 8 6 10	XXXCX
7 − 7 − 8 5 7	XXO
5 11 6 5 − 6 8 10 8 2 11 7	XO
9 8 3 10 9 − 6 7	XO
7 − 8 7	XO
6 10 8 8 8 11 10 7	O
7 − 4 3 5 7	XO
7 − 9 3 6 10 5 9 − 7 − 4 12 8 7	XXXO
5 7	O
11 − 9 4 8 4 8 11 11 8 4 8 3 6 5 8 7	XO
4 7	O
8 6 4 8 − 10 5 12 7	XO
7 − 7 − 10 6 6 5 10 − 11 − 2 − 6 4 4 10 6 −	XXXX2X
7 − 5 8 5 − 9 10 5 11 7	XXO
7 − 8 7	XO
7 − 9 8 2 9 − 9 6 6 9 − 7 − 6 6 − 6 9 6 − 10 7	XXXXXXO
4 6 10 5 10 8 6 11 9 11 6 5 10 7	O
9 6 10 7	O
3 − 7 − 3 − 9 7	CXCO
4 5 5 5 11 10 6 8 9 7	O
8 7	O
7 − 7 − 6 7	XXO
6 7	O
7 − 9 4 9 − 2 − 3 − 7 − 12 − 9 6 5 7	XX2CXBO
3 − 9 7	CO
4 7	O
6 6 − 6 8 8 9 5 7	XO
7 − 8 11 7	XO
7 − 6 5 7	XO
11 − 10 7	XO
5 3 9 5 − 8 7	XO
8 9 10 9 8 − 9 10 5 7	XO

10 4 10 − 5 8 7	XO
7 − 5 2 6 8 4 6 9 8 11 6 8 5 − 5 8 7	XXO
8 7	O
6 11 11 9 6 − 6 7	XO
9 7	O
6 8 7	O
8 3 3 10 7	O
6 5 9 10 7	O
11 − 3 − 7 − 5 6 8 5 − 8 11 5 9 7	XCXXO
9 10 8 5 7	O
4 8 8 8 2 3 7	O
7 − 12 − 10 7	XBO
9 5 7	O
5 10 10 8 7	O
4 4 − 9 7	XO
4 6 3 4 − 7 − 8 8 − 6 3 7	XXXO
3 − 6 10 8 9 4 5 8 10 10 4 6 − 3 − 8 8 −	CXCX
9 6 11 11 7	O
6 7	O
9 7	O
4 8 12 7	O
8 7	O
7 − 4 2 5 7	XO
7 − 5 9 11 10 7	XO
8 7	O
6 8 5 6 − 11 − 5 7	XXO
6 9 11 6 − 6 7	XO
9 9 − 3 − 9 12 8 5 7	XCO
9 4 6 3 5 6 8 7	O
11 − 9 3 2 6 7	XO
5 11 5 − 10 10 − 5 9 9 2 7	XXO
6 6 − 5 2 4 4 4 7	XO
3 − 2 − 7 − 7 − 7 − 6 8 8 4 4 3 11 8 12 9 6 −	C2XXXX
11 − 2 − 6 3 8 10 8 7	X2O
11 − 9 4 3 8 7	XO
10 4 4 12 9 8 6 2 11 7	O
8 10 6 10 6 3 6 4 7	O

°°[∞]□□°□□□□□°□°□□□□°□°□□□□□°□°□□□□■□□□□°□°^{∞∞}□□°□°□□□□□□°□°□□□°□°□□□□□°□°□□□°□°□°□□□°□°^{∞∞∞∞}□□°□°□□□

2 − 6 6 − 6 3 3 6 − 6 10 5 7	2XXO
12 − 6 10 11 6 − 7 − 4 3 9 6 7	BXXO
9 6 6 4 6 4 6 10 6 11 7	O
5 4 9 8 7	O
12 − 9 4 3 4 8 6 12 9 − 4 11 5 6 7	BXO
4 4 − 7 − 9 5 9 − 10 6 2 7	XXXO
8 9 3 9 9 7	O
5 8 7	O
3 − 8 7	CO
3 − 6 7	CO
5 3 8 6 7	O
4 10 7	O
5 10 6 11 10 10 4 8 9 12 5 − 9 11 5 9 − 9 9 − 9 7	XXXO
5 7	O
8 7	O
7 − 4 6 12 7	XO
8 8 − 4 8 7	XO
11 − 3 − 7 − 10 6 9 6 4 5 5 7	XCXO
9 5 6 7	O
9 2 10 6 4 11 7	O
7 − 5 6 7	XO
7 − 7 − 6 10 6 − 5 4 8 12 4 8 3 8 4 8 5 −	XXXX
8 8 − 2 − 6 7	X2O
10 5 10 − 3 − 3 − 12 − 10 10 − 9 9 − 10 8	XCCBX
6 9 9 9 9 7	XO
3 − 6 7	CO
7 − 8 7	XO
5 7	O
7 − 8 7	XO
9 9 − 4 10 9 7	XO
4 4 − 10 10 − 10 11 7	XXO
9 9 − 12 − 4 8 4 − 7 − 8 4 7	XBXXO
7 − 10 8 11 4 9 11 11 9 9 8 8 9 5 8 10 − 8 6 6 7	XXO
9 4 7	O
4 10 7	O
10 3 7	O

6 **10** 7	O
9 7	O
9 6 8 7	O
10 10 − 7 − 11 − 10 2 10 − 7 − 11 − 8 9 **10** 6	XXXXXX
10 5 6 7	O
8 7	O
9 7	O
9 9 − 4 8 4 − 10 3 5 11 8 7	XXO
4 6 7	O
9 10 6 8 9 − 10 3 5 7	XO
12 − 6 9 6 − 4 7	BXO
9 8 9 − 6 4 5 11 3 3 5 7	XO
8 4 7	O
9 7	O
5 6 6 7	O
2 − 9 7	2O
4 7	O
5 8 10 6 5 − 4 8 7	XO
7 − 8 6 11 11 11 10 8 − 3 − 3 − 7 − 7 − 11 −	XXCCXXX
7 − 6 5 12 12 5 5 9 3 10 11 6 − 5 7	XXO
8 10 7	O
6 4 9 8 8 9 4 8 8 6 − 7 − 10 7	XXO
5 11 9 7	O
6 7	O
8 6 10 3 5 6 7	O
2 − 8 7	2O
10 10 − 3 − 5 10 7	XCO
6 8 6 − 5 9 7	XO
9 9 − 7 − 3 − 4 7	XXCO
9 9 − 5 8 9 6 5 − 3 − 6 9 2 7	XXCO
7 − 10 6 8 5 9 9 8 8 7	XO
9 **10** 9 − 4 9 5 6 9 3 8 9 7	XO
7 − 3 − 5 7	XCO
9 6 4 5 7	O
6 8 10 2 5 6 − 7 − 5 10 4 3 7	XXO
7 − 5 3 10 5 − 7 − 4 8 7	XXXO
6 5 4 4 5 5 7	O

11 − 6 2 2 8 9 11 9 9 7	XO
5 4 **10** 5 − 6 11 4 9 8 4 4 7	XO
11 − 12 − 5 5 − 8 9 9 11 7	XBXO
3 − 5 6 9 8 9 7	CO
10 5 6 **10** − 7 − 5 6 5 − 8 5 5 9 8 − 7 − 7 −	XXXXXX
8 8 − 9 9 − 7 − 9 5 9 − 8 8 − 9 5 7	XXXXXO
8 7	O
6 10 8 11 7	O
11 − 7 − 5 6 7	XXO
8 9 5 12 3 7	O
2 − 8 8 − 7 − 6 7	2XXO
7 − 10 4 6 6 2 9 5 3 **10** − 5 9 6 7	XXO
9 3 4 6 10 6 8 5 10 11 7	O
10 5 8 6 11 10 − 7 − 9 4 9 − 11 − 4 8 7	XXXXO
8 6 **10** 5 7	O
8 4 2 5 4 6 4 5 4 5 8 − 3 − 6 **10** 7	XCO
9 8 7	O
11 − 5 7	XO
4 8 5 8 4 − 7 − 12 − 6 7	XXBO
7 − 7 − 6 9 5 8 7	XXO
11 − 7 − 4 3 7	XXO
8 4 3 6 7	O
8 11 8 − 12 − 6 11 9 5 8 6 − 5 9 8 6 **10** 12 8 7	XBXO
9 4 9 − 10 9 8 9 11 4 8 6 8 9 11 12 6 8 **6** 11 7	XO
3 − 8 12 8 − 5 8 5 − 8 12 7	CXXO
8 12 6 7	O
10 8 5 7	O
8 4 **10 10** 7	O
8 7	O
4 7	O
9 7	O
5 4 7	O
9 6 4 4 5 10 4 4 9 − 7 − 10 6 9 10 − 6 8 2 6 −	XXXX
4 12 11 9 6 4 − 8 **10** 4 7	XO
9 4 10 5 6 6 11 8 4 8 10 11 8 7	O
9 5 7	O

6 7	O
2 − 9 4 6 3 4 5 10 4 6 8 9 − 4 4 − 5 10 8 12 5 − 11 − 8 4 6 10 7	2XXX XO
4 12 11 7	O
10 5 11 5 7	O
7 − 8 3 7	XO
4 2 8 9 3 7	O
7 − 11 − 5 4 11 6 6 11 5 − 8 6 9 6 10 5 5 5 4 8 − 6 8 8 7	XXXX O
8 6 5 10 3 7	O
10 6 6 8 3 11 11 7	O
7 − 2 − 4 8 10 2 2 8 7	X2O
10 7	O
8 8 − 7 − 8 11 5 4 2 11 7	XXO
7 − 7 − 9 9 − 4 11 11 5 6 8 9 8 4 − 6 6 − 9 5 10 10 6 11 6 7	XXXXX O
6 8 7	O
9 4 8 9 − 9 2 5 9 − 2 − 6 9 9 7	XX2O
7 − 10 6 12 9 3 2 5 5 8 2 4 8 8 4 10 − 8 5 6 12 11 5 7	XX O
6 3 7	O
9 5 8 11 8 7	O
4 3 7	O
7 − 6 6 − 6 6 − 8 4 9 7	XXXO
7 − 9 7	XO
11 − 7 − 10 10 − 5 6 7	XXXO
4 11 6 9 10 7	O
7 − 7 − 5 11 8 2 10 10 7	XXO
7 − 5 8 7	XO
5 8 10 9 7	O
7 − 8 6 10 7	XO
6 10 6 − 10 7	XO
6 4 7	O
11 − 5 9 4 7	XO
6 5 8 9 4 5 8 9 5 9 5 5 11 6 − 10 7	XO
9 6 3 10 5 6 11 3 2 8 9 − 10 5 5 11 6 9 9 5 8 4 2 7	X O

7 – 3 – 9 4 8 9 – 6 6 – 7 – 9 7	XCXXXO
7 – 8 8 – 8 12 10 4 5 4 6 11 10 5 9 9 9 6 10	XXX
3 11 10 5 8 – 8 4 8 – 9 8 4 5 3 8 3 9 – 8 8 –	XXX
6 5 5 3 11 9 3 7	O
4 6 5 8 5 7	O
7 – 7 – 6 5 4 11 7	XXO
5 9 7	O
5 10 9 10 12 7	O
8 11 3 5 6 7	O
9 7	O
7 – 6 12 9 7	XO
5 10 9 9 5 – 10 10 – 8 6 9 5 3 6 11 4 6 9 6 8 –	XXX
12 – 4 9 8 8 11 6 9 9 10 9 7	BO
6 12 6 – 10 4 7	XO
9 6 7	O
4 7	O
8 5 10 4 4 12 10 5 9 4 9 9 11 7	O
9 5 11 3 7	O
7 – 7 – 5 8 4 4 10 9 5 – 12 – 3 – 5 8 8 4 7	XXXBCO
7 – 9 8 9 – 10 6 3 7	XXO
4 7	O
8 11 5 11 6 5 10 5 9 8 – 7 – 7 – 6 5 5 7	XXXO
6 7	O
8 9 10 11 7	O
9 8 9 – 8 9 6 11 8 – 7 – 6 10 5 5 4 5 4 8 4 11 3 7	XXXO
8 10 6 7	O
6 8 5 8 4 5 7	O
8 8 – 11 – 8 6 5 4 5 2 10 10 6 3 5 4 8 –	XXX
6 6 – 6 7	XO
10 7	O
10 8 4 3 7	O
7 – 2 – 6 2 6 – 8 3 6 8 – 5 9 7	X2XXO
8 5 8 – 9 6 10 6 10 4 4 7	XO
6 8 12 10 10 4 4 6 – 4 4 – 10 6 7	XXO
9 9 – 8 8 – 4 12 6 9 7	XXO
5 3 7	O

8 9 10 10 8 − 7 − 8 5 10 5 10 11 6 5 10 12 8 −	XXX
8 12 5 8 − 5 6 7	XO
9 4 10 7	O
9 8 8 7	O
8 4 11 7	O
11 − 6 11 5 9 10 4 7	XO
9 10 3 8 5 9 − 7 − 6 5 6 − 7 − 4 8 8 6 7	XXXXO
10 6 5 3 5 8 7	O
6 6 − 6 7	XO
2 − 7 − 6 5 8 6 − 2 − 2 − 7 − 12 −	2XX22XB
3 − 6 6 − 4 7	CXO
7 − 9 6 12 9 − 7 − 4 5 9 5 6 6 11 7	XXXO
5 5 − 8 10 9 3 6 4 8 − 6 5 9 4 8 10 8 7	XXO
3 − 5 6 8 5 − 10 6 5 6 5 7	CXO
2 − 3 − 4 12 11 3 9 8 5 4 − 9 5 10 8 6 6 11 7	2CXO
11 − 5 10 8 6 3 4 5 − 6 9 3 11 5 11 8 5 9 10 7	XXO
6 11 9 6 − 7 − 9 9 − 7 − 5 6 5 − 11 − 8 10 10 8 −	XXXXXX
7 − 5 4 3 5 − 6 6 − 6 12 5 7	XXXXO
9 4 7	O
10 8 4 5 9 6 8 10 − 6 8 6 − 9 8 5 5 9 −	XXX
7 − 6 4 5 8 8 7	XO
3 − 8 3 4 5 6 6 4 10 5 5 8 − 8 4 3 12 5 9 9	CXX
9 4 5 6 9 12 4 8 − 7 − 8 5 7	XO
10 8 8 11 9 3 7	O
10 7	O
5 8 8 7	O
4 5 9 7	O
11 − 7 − 4 6 3 5 5 4 − 9 8 9 − 7 − 3 −	XXXX
4 3 6 8 7	XCO
4 5 2 11 9 8 5 8 5 10 12 3 7	O

9 6 4 4 8 9 — 5 6 6 5 — 7 — 8 3 10 7	XXXO
9 4 5 6 6 10 4 6 7	O
8 2 5 6 11 6 9 5 9 7	O
6 11 10 3 9 8 7	O
6 5 8 8 8 7	O
4 6 11 11 8 6 7	O
7 — 7 — 6 5 7	XXO
7 — 9 10 5 10 6 9 — 12 — 5 9 4 8 8 4 6 2 9 3	XXB
6 6 11 8 5 — 6 6 — 8 7	XXO
8 8 — 4 4 — 9 8 10 7	XXO
6 7	O
6 9 7	O
8 6 8 — 8 2 9 5 7	XO
7 — 4 9 6 8 7	XO
8 6 5 7	O
11 — 8 5 11 8 — 9 7	XXO
2 — 5 7	2O
8 5 5 7	O
8 8 — 9 8 7	XO
3 — 7 — 7 — 3 — 7 — 9 7	CXXCXO
4 7	O
5 7	O
7 — 5 5 — 3 — 2 — 6 9 7	XXC2O
6 7	O
9 7	O
3 — 12 — 5 6 7	CBO
10 6 10 — 6 10 8 4 6 — 5 11 10 8 6 4 8 6 5 —	XXX
9 10 5 8 8 6 7	O
2 — 5 3 9 9 5 — 10 7	2XO
7 — 6 7	XO
2 — 7 — 9 11 7	2XO
8 10 4 2 12 6 8 — 2 — 10 3 6 5 8 10 — 2 —	X2X2
7 — 6 7	XO
5 7	O
3 — 5 5 — 11 — 7 — 6 7	CXXXO
7 — 10 3 6 7	XO

8 6 9 5 6 7	O
10 8 **10** − 7 − 3 − 12 − 9 6 5 4 4 **10** 5	XXCB
6 6 9 − 5 9 7	XO
8 5 8 − 5 7	XO
5 **10** 6 9 8 **10** 4 **10** 7	O
6 6 − 11 − 9 11 7	XXO
10 8 4 6 8 5 9 8 11 6 5 12 6 10 − 6 8 9 6 − 7 −	XXX
7 − 6 4 11 3 10 2 5 6 − 7 − 7 − 6 **10** 9 9 7	XXXXO
8 3 **10** 8 − 3 − 7 − 3 − 7 − 11 − 9 2	XCXCXX
8 8 8 5 6 7	O
4 12 7	O
12 − 4 9 **10** 9 3 6 7	BO
4 8 9 9 **10** 4 − 7 − 7 − 7 − 10 11 4 5 6 8 8 7	XXXXO
6 9 9 5 8 6 − 7 − 4 9 12 9 5 7	XXO
4 **10** 5 4 − 8 3 3 7	XO
9 6 5 7	O
3 − 7 − 6 7	CXO
8 6 6 3 **10** 7	O
8 7	O
5 7	O
7 − 11 − 8 7	XXO
6 9 6 − 11 − 9 9 − 9 8 12 5 4 9 − 6 6 −	XXXXX
9 8 3 11 6 8 3 7	O
7 − 11 − 5 12 6 8 3 **10** 4 8 3 4 4 4 5 − 7 −	XXXX
5 6 11 11 11 6 8 4 6 11 7	O
6 7	O
3 − 8 8 − **10** 9 8 5 9 7	CXO
4 8 5 3 6 5 9 3 7	O
3 − 7 − 9 9 − 7 − 11 −6 6 −	CXXXXX
8 8 − 5 7	XO
4 9 9 6 4 − 7 − 4 6 8 5 9 6 3 **10** 8 7	XXO
9 8 4 5 7	O

7 – 7 – 7 – 8 8 – 7 – 7 – 4 9 10 7	XXXXXXO
6 8 8 4 7	O
9 9 – 8 6 10 7	XO
9 7	O
6 6 – 3 – 7 – 7 – 11 – 9 5 7	XCXXXO
10 5 6 5 9 8 9 8 9 7	O
4 7	O
5 9 4 11 5 – 8 5 6 8 – 11 – 8 8 –	XXX
10 11 8 6 8 5 12 6 8 8 7	XO
6 10 6 – 10 11 8 7	XO
7 – 10 8 9 7	XO
10 9 10 – 10 10 – 9 9 – 11 – 8 8 – 9 5 7	XXXXXO
8 9 7	O
7 – 11 – 7 – 8 6 7	XXXO
7 – 8 9 7	XO
4 5 7	O
6 3 3 8 7	O
7 – 5 4 7	XO
9 7	O
8 8 – 7 – 10 5 10 – 9 7	XXXO
8 11 7	O
5 7	O
11 – 8 4 6 8 – 8 9 7	XXO
7 – 10 7	XO
10 8 3 7	O
10 11 6 7	O
5 7	O
6 7	O
8 10 8 – 6 5 11 5 9 5 10 5 7	XO
10 6 4 4 8 5 2 5 7	O
7 – 3 – 7 – 4 7	XCXO
7 – 4 3 5 12 11 6 7	XO
8 11 6 3 9 9 3 10 10 7	O
7 – 7 – 6 8 8 5 7	XXO
4 9 10 7	O

10 10 – 6 10 8 6 – 2 – 3 – 12 –	**XX2CB**
4 8 8 3 5 4 – 8 3 5 9 3 10 6 5 9 2 8 – 10 8 7	**XXO**
5 5 – 5 6 8 12 7	**XO**
9 **6** 6 11 6 4 6 7	**O**
6 10 7	**O**
7 – 8 8 – 2 – 6 8 4 2 10 7	**XX2O**
8 6 3 6 6 10 9 9 11 6 5 9 7	**O**
9 8 6 11 4 5 7	**O**
2 – 6 3 5 7	**2O**
8 7	**O**
8 3 6 8 – 9 4 8 12 6 4 **4** 9 – 10 7	**XXO**
8 7	**O**
10 10 – 9 2 5 11 7	**XO**
4 7	**O**
3 – 6 2 9 9 4 2 2 6 – 2 – 8 7	**CX2O**
5 **6 8** 7	**O**
6 6 – 10 12 8 8 5 9 5 9 3 5 6 10 – 5 8 7	**XXO**
11 – 5 7	**XO**
9 11 7	**O**
4 9 7	**O**
7 – 11 – 2 – 5 2 7	**XX2O**
8 8 – 11 – 8 7	**XXO**
11 – 5 6 2 8 5 – 11 – 4 5 4 – 7 –	**XXXXX**
9 8 5 6 7	**O**
5 9 7	**O**
9 7	**O**
9 5 6 5 7	**O**
8 7	**O**
9 5 6 8 **10** 4 6 11 3 6 6 7	**O**
8 6 6 5 6 9 11 6 8 – 7 – 5 8 7	**XXO**
8 7	**O**
10 8 3 6 7	**O**
7 – 6 5 6 – 7 – 5 9 4 9 10 5 – 8 3 11 10 10 7	**XXXXO**
2 – 5 9 10 5 – 7 – 5 11 2 8 4 7	**2XXO**
2 – 9 8 11 5 5 5 2 4 5 8 6 7	**2O**
8 9 8 – 3 – 10 5 9 2 6 7	**XCO**
8 8 – 10 7	**XO**

5 6 5 − 4 10 8 2 11 7	XO
8 7	O
12 − 5 6 5 − 5 7	BXO
5 3 **10** 5 − 7 − 8 7	XXO
6 6 − 6 6 − 6 11 8 10 4 3 8 5 3 **10** 7	XXO
10 6 7	O
6 7	O
2 − 5 11 5 − 3 − 5 6 9 4 4 4 6 6 7	2XCO
7 − 2 − 4 6 **10** 8 11 6 7	X2O
7 − 8 8 − 7 − 4 3 3 7	XXXO
7 − 7 − 9 4 10 12 4 7	XXO
2 − 5 5 − 12 − 7 − 9 5 10 11 9 − 5 9 7	2XBXXO
7 − 8 6 7	XO
9 4 7	O
2 − 3 − 3 − 6 4 4 7	2CCO
7 − 6 8 3 10 6 − 11 − 9 7	XXXO
4 5 7	O
7 − 4 2 11 11 4 − 4 11 6 7	XXO
4 3 8 9 4 − 8 7	XO
7 − 5 4 10 5 − 7 − 4 9 6 2 4 − 7 −	XXXXX
4 11 11 8 3 4 − 4 7	XO
4 8 9 4 − 6 9 10 5 6 − 3 − 7 − 2 −	XXCX2
8 4 5 3 9 4 4 7	O
9 5 7	O
7 − 4 9 9 4 − 8 3 8 − 3 − 10 3 9 10 − 10 6 7	XXXCXO
7 − 9 3 11 7	XO
5 3 7	O
4 5 9 3 5 12 7	O
4 4 − 5 7	XO

8 5 8 − 2 − 2 − 8 11 3 9 12 8 − 3 −	X22XC
4 1 2 8 5 9 7	O
11 − 7 − 10 4 12 7	XXO
10 9 6 6 7	O
10 9 7	O
2 − 8 7	2O
10 5 5 8 9 **10** − 7 − 11 − 8 10 **8** − 3 − 5 5 −	XXXXCX
7 − 11 − 9 6 7	XXO
6 10 7	O
5 5 − 4 3 8 6 8 8 7	XO
4 5 4 − 7 − 3 − 7 − 7 − 7 − 5 7	XXCXXXO
4 12 9 4 − 4 9 7	XO
3 − 10 7	CO
7 − 5 4 6 7	XO
5 7	O
8 8 − 7 − 8 6 8 − 4 7	XXXO
7 − 5 7	XO
7 − 5 9 7	XO
6 12 3 9 4 8 4 10 3 7	O
6 3 3 3 9 7	O
9 7	O
10 7	O
4 10 **4** − 6 8 9 5 7	XO
6 8 5 8 7	O
4 5 5 8 12 7	O
8 8 − 6 5 11 7	XO
6 3 6 − 7 − 10 6 5 3 7	XXO
9 4 10 8 5 8 7	O
4 5 5 8 9 2 12 3 3 7	O
6 4 6 − 7 − 4 11 10 6 5 9 10 11 9 11 8 9	XXX
6 9 10 5 4 − 11 − 7 − 7 − **10** 11 7	XXXO
3 − 7 − 6 7	CXO
8 8 − 5 5 − 9 10 12 11 4 6 9 − 6 5 11 11	XXX
4 **10 6** − 6 8 8 8 7	XO
7 − 10 8 7	XO
10 6 2 7	O

7 − 7 − 9 7	XXO
8 7	O
10 7	O
9 5 10 5 6 8 5 9 − 5 4 9 7	XO
9 7	O
11 − 6 6 − 10 10 − 9 3 10 7	XXXO
6 6 − 5 7	XO
9 7	O
10 5 8 6 2 6 11 7	O
8 5 7	O
5 11 3 5 − 8 8 − 8 6 4 8 − 6 7	XXXO
6 10 11 9 7	O
10 7	O
8 9 6 7	O
5 2 8 11 6 11 12 5 − 7 − 11 − 8 5 11 10 7	XXXO
4 12 6 3 6 8 6 8 9 6 4 − 8 8 − 8 5 5 7	XXO
7 − 4 3 5 8 9 10 2 5 4 − 9 11 7	XXO
7 − 10 3 5 10 − 6 8 5 3 8 7	XXO
10 5 5 7	O
8 8 − 8 3 8 − 9 4 8 7	XXO
5 3 3 3 10 9 6 12 11 11 8 6 6 8 2 11 5 − 7 −	XX
3 − 3 − 5 7	CCO
8 11 7	O
8 6 7	O
8 11 10 5 8 − 7 − 9 11 2 4 8 7	XXO
5 11 7	O
9 11 5 7	O
9 8 11 7	O
11 − 10 5 5 9 12 11 10 − 11 − 6 11 5 7	XXXO
6 4 6 − 5 5 − 11 − 6 8 9 7	XXXO
5 6 8 8 9 4 6 8 5 − 7 − 5 7	XXO
5 10 5 − 6 9 8 4 11 7	XO
8 11 7	O
9 3 3 7	O
4 1 10 8 4 − 8 6 8 − 11 − 10 3 9 6 10 −	XXXX
8 10 6 6 8 − 9 10 8 6 7	XO

7 − 3 − 2 − 3 − 7 − 8 6 9 7	XC2CXO
9 11 5 7	O
11 − 2 − 5 9 5 − 4 3 9 7	X2XO
6 8 4 4 3 11 11 10 10 8 6 − 6 11 5 3 5 3 8	X
5 8 5 9 8 10 11 5 11 7	O
8 5 4 9 5 5 4 7	O
6 11 6 − 7 − 8 7	XXO
12 − 5 7	BO
7 − 8 12 12 2 9 11 6 6 8 − 10 7	XXO
9 9 − 9 9 − 4 8 9 7	XXO
6 2 10 8 6 − 7 − 11 − 2 − 11 − 11 − 10 7	XXX2XXO
7 − 5 5 − 10 11 4 8 4 5 4 6 6 3 6 10 −	XXX
11 − 4 8 11 4 − 9 3 7	XXO
8 11 8 − 7 − 2 − 7 − 6 6 − 6 7	XX2XXO
9 6 8 9 − 5 3 7	XO
5 10 4 8 4 7	O
3 − 12 − 7 − 10 8 11 11 8 11 9 5 7	CBXO
6 4 4 9 9 9 7	O
2 − 11 − 8 7	2XO
3 − 7 − 7 − 12 − 6 7	CXXBO
5 5 − 9 11 6 9 − 8 12 4 6 11 5 6 11 6 9 6 9 7	XXO
7 − 7 − 3 − 5 6 7	XXCO
11 − 10 7	XO
4 5 4 − 8 10 10 6 9 2 5 6 8 − 11 − 8 5 9 5 9 7	XXXO
5 9 12 3 12 4 4 12 9 10 11 5 − 4 97	XO
8 7	O
5 10 4 3 4 6 6 4 11 6 10 10 4 4 8 8 10 2 7	O
4 9 6 9 7	O
6 7	O
4 8 8 6 6 7	O

7 – 12 – 4 9 5 6 6 7	XBO
5 9 10 5 – 6 11 5 10 6 – 10 2 8 5 8 4 10 – 4 6 7	XXXO
5 3 6 11 7	O
6 10 10 5 12 6 – 9 9 – 5 11 7	XXO
4 10 11 8 9 11 8 8 11 5 11 7	O
3 – 7 – 5 11 7	CXO
7 – 2 – 5 6 3 3 5 – 7 – 5 7	X2XXO
7 – 8 10 9 9 11 7	XO
7 – 6 9 6 – 8 5 8 – 4 11 3 5 6 11 9 6 8 6 9 5	XXX
10 5 6 2 11 10 8 5 5 9 9 8 6 9 8 2 8 11 9	
6 8 9 6 9 10 8 10 3 6 10 7	O
7 – 8 8 – 9 11 10 9 – 8 5 5 6 11 10 3 6 8 –	XXXX
7 – 7 – 9 7	XXO
8 5 6 7	O
8 6 7	O
7 – 6 6 – 9 4 8 9 – 6 4 9 7	XXXO
6 10 12 2 11 6 – 7 – 11 – 12 – 6 12 7	XXXBO
8 2 7	O
7 – 8 6 8 – 7 – 11 – 6 9 5 2 8 7	XXXXO
4 6 4 – 6 9 9 8 3 4 4 5 7	XO
7 – 12 – 9 6 10 10 8 4 8 2 4 11 5 5 11 7	XBO
9 11 5 10 7	O
7 – 7 – 5 9 7	XXO
3 – 5 11 10 6 4 6 5 – 5 7	CXO
5 9 5 – 9 8 10 9 – 5 4 4 8 7	XXO
3 – 6 8 4 4 10 6 – 9 7	CXO
7 – 6 4 8 6 – 6 9 10 8 7	XXO
8 11 2 10 11 5 7	O
7 – 3 – 3 – 10 11 10 – 7 – 5 3 8 6 12 9	XCCXX
10 6 3 11 9 7	O
4 2 11 7	O
5 7	O

10 7	O
4 9 7	O
10 6 6 6 8 7	O
9 5 10 6 9 − 10 6 5 10 − 10 8 4 5 10 − 7 − 5 7	XXXXO
7 − 8 5 10 7	XO
9 12 4 7	O
3 − 9 4 7	CO
8 7	O
11 − 7 − 8 7	XXO
10 12 6 5 8 8 10 − 5 6 8 9 6 3 6 7	XO
7 − 8 10 4 9 5 5 7	XO
8 12 6 6 11 3 6 7	O
7 − 7 − 5 12 8 9 7	XXO
6 10 10 4 3 6 − 5 7	XO
3 − 3 − 10 5 10 − 7 − 7 − 6 5 9 12 5 5 11 7	CCXXXO
5 5 − 5 7	XO
6 3 3 6 − 7 − 10 5 7	XXO
7 − 5 12 10 5 − 2 − 9 11 9 − 7 − 10 8 9 10 −	XX2XXX
7 − 3 − 5 4 9 7	XCO
3 − 7 − 7 − 7 − 2 − 9 6 3 8 7	CXXX2O
5 8 2 4 9 2 7	O
5 10 7	O
6 11 9 10 9 7	O
12 − 10 9 4 5 5 4 2 7	BO
9 6 10 5 3 4 8 5 10 8 5 2 4 5 4 4 4 5 9 − 8 5 3 7	XO
10 8 10 − 8 8 − 5 7	XXO
5 3 8 6 8 11 12 3 6 9 6 8 3 12 7	O
7 − 2 − 4 5 7	X2O
5 3 8 10 6 4 7	O
4 5 9 8 9 5 5 10 5 7	O
9 4 2 12 9 − 4 5 3 9 7	XO
8 7	O
10 11 5 4 6 6 6 7	O
7 − 3 − 6 2 4 7	XCO
8 6 4 5 10 7	O

11 − 88 − 3 − 10 5 6 7	XXCO
2 − 7 − 6 7	2XO
5 12 10 9 9 7⁻	O
6 2 8 3 5 6 − 11 − 6 11 8 7	XXO
2 − 12 − 88 − 7 − 9 8 9 − 7 − 3 −	2BXXXXC
12 − 7 − 4 3 5 9 6 2 5 9 10 6 10 6 10 10	BX
10 5 3 7	O
11 − 6 8 8 6 − 12 − 10 10 − 6 8 10 6 − 8 10 7	XXBXXO
10 5 4 8 11 11 8 2 6 9 9 8 7	O
9 8 7	O
5 3 6 7	O
6 10 6 − 7 − 5 7	XXO
12 − 8 4 7	BO
6 4 3 9 7	O
8 10 4 8 − 10 4 6 8 7	XO
11 − 5 4 7	XO
6 5 9 10 7	O
7 − 10 8 9 8 8 5 9 9 9 12 10 − 8 8 − 7 − 3 −	XXXXC
7 − 7 − 10 5 9 5 4 6 6 8 4 11 4 8 10 −	XXX
12 − 7 − 3 − 7 − 8 5 7	BXCXO
7 − 6 6 − 11 − 6 5 7	XXXO
5 7	O
5 3 11 6 3 11 7	O
10 11 9 5 4 6 4 8 6 11 9 8 9 9 4 9 6 10 −	X
10 5 2 5 3 5 7	O
4 2 7	O
11 − 6 7	XO
11 − 11 − 7 − 9 8 8 9 − 9 7	XXXXO
8 5 5 7	O
7 − 5 9 11 5 − 4 10 8 10 5 8 9 4 − 2 − 5 12 9 7	XXX2O
8 10 6 6 7	O
8 6 5 7	O
8 4 4 11 4 5 5 6 4 9 4 6 12 3 9 9 4 5 7	O
3 − 4 7	CO
11 − 3 − 8 11 11 5 4 10 8 − 6 9 10 4 9 11	XCX
5 2 5 5 7	O
7 − 6 7	XO

7 − 6 7	XO
5 7	O
8 6 **10** 6 7	O
10 7	O
11 − 9 11 9 − 6 11 8 8 7	XXO
8 9 7	O
4 7	O
3 − 7 − 7 − 4 11 8 4 − 5 6 5 − 8 10 5 9 3 4 7	CXXXXO
8 9 5 6 4 6 6 8 − 7 − 7 − 9 6 9 − 5 5 −	XXXXX
10 2 2 8 9 6 6 8 6 4 12 6 2 9 7	O
7 − 12 − 6 2 **10** 7	XBO
8 4 6 2 9 10 8 − 7 − 9 7	XXO
6 6 − 11 − 9 11 7	XXO
8 9 8 − 5 9 8 7	XO
4 5 5 9 8 3 5 7	O
9 3 6 2 10 4 8 7	O
7 − 4 8 9 7	XO
7 − 5 8 8 7	XO
4 8 5 5 9 8 9 7	O
9 8 8 5 5 5 3 12 7	O
9 10 3 8 2 3 9 − 8 11 9 6 7	XO
5 8 4 3 10 11 6 9 11 4 6 9 7	O
4 11 3 6 8 8 6 6 7	O
10 3 8 4 7	O
10 9 8 11 9 6 4 6 3 7	O
7 − 8 7	XO
4 4 − 7 − 8 7	XXO
8 7	O
11 − 10 7	XO
8 6 4 8 − 9 8 6 5 6 8 10 3 5 12 4 8 2 4 8 9 −	XX
8 4 11 6 6 3 9 4 4 4 3 6 9 10 8 − 4 5 4 −	XX
12 − 11 − 6 6 − 7 − 8 9 7	BXXXO
3 − 10 12 9 8 7	CO
5 8 5 − 4 11 11 7	XO
8 6 8 − 6 2 4 9 8 7	XO
8 9 10 6 9 10 5 10 4 3 10 10 7	O

°□□□□□°°□□□□□°°□□□□°□°°□□□□□°□°°°■□°□°□°□°□□□°□°□□□°□□□□□°□°°□□°°□□°□°°□□□□°°□□□°°□°□°■□°°□□□°□°□□

4 3 6 7	O
5 **10** 8 4 2 12 7	O
7 − 3 − 7 − 3 − 7 − 3 − 3 − 12 − 3 − 7 −	XCXCXC
8 5 7	CBCXO
3 − 11 − 5 5 − 6 6 − 11 − 5 8 8 7	CXXXXO
8 7	O
9 7	O
4 3 **8 10** 9 11 8 7	O
7 − 4 6 5 11 11 12 7	XO
6 6 − 6 4 10 5 4 8 6 − 9 7	XXO
7 − 10 3 11 9 6 6 8 9 8 9 5 3 6 8 5 6 9 6	X
4 6 8 2 5 8 3 9 7	O
5 11 12 7	O
2 − 8 6 8 − 6 2 5 9 11 6 − 11 − 5 4 4 7	2XXXO
5 12 9 7	O
11 − 5 7	XO
8 8 − 2 − 11 − 7 − **10 10** − 8 9 11 5 9 6 4	X2XXX
9 5 4 11 7	O
4 7	O
6 7	O
2 − 7 − 10 4 7	2XO
5 7	O
9 4 7	O
6 12 10 9 9 11 9 9 10 **6** − 11 − 8 3 3 8 − 6 3 5	XXXX
10 12 3 4 3 5 9 6 − 3 − 8 9 9 7	CO
4 10 7	O
6 2 6 − 6 5 5 5 7	XO
6 11 **10** 6 − 7 − 5 11 8 8 4 11 6 7	XXO
3 − 3 − 10 7	CCO
7 − 8 5 7	XO
4 6 8 6 7	O
8 7	O
8 6 5 6 4 10 8 − 7 − 8 12 10 **8** − 11 −	XXXX
10 3 9 11 9 7	O
8 6 **10** 11 5 5 8 − 7 − 10 6 2 9 8 7	XXO
7 − 4 7	XO
3 − 9 7	CO

7 − 4 9 2 9 8 5 5 10 5 2 8 9 6 8 6 3 5	XX
8 10 9 10 3 10 4 − 6 11 7	O
10 8 8 8 3 6 10 − 6 11 3 7	XO
7 − 9 4 5 8 6 7	XO
8 2 7	O
8 3 3 5 12 2 7	O
9 5 8 8 6 6 10 3 6 7	O
9 5 3 6 9 − 9 9 − 7 − 9 11 3 7	XXXO
2 − 7 − 2 − 9 7	2X2O
5 5 − 6 8 8 3 6 − 8 8 − 10 9 10 − 9 8 9 −	XXXXX
7 − 7 − 6 9 9 6 − 7 − 6 6 − 9 6 7	XXXXXO
4 6 4 − 11 − 9 9 − 9 7	XXXO
7 − 9 7	XO
7 − 3 − 3 − 3 − 4 8 7	XCCCO
8 2 10 3 6 7	O
2 − 5 9 4 4 7	2O
3 − 10 12 3 6 4 6 8 4 6 10 − 8 2 7	CXO
8 5 7	O
6 12 4 10 9 7	O
5 7	O
5 9 4 9 6 5 − 7 − 5 9 10 9 4 11 10 6 10 5 −	XXX
9 4 9 − 9 4 3 7	XO
6 8 7	O
8 3 8 − 7 − 4 5 5 6 6 8 3 5 10 6 4 −	XXX
8 10 8 − 6 7	XO
8 7	O
10 11 7	O
6 5 7	O
3 − 3 − 11 − 4 3 8 10 5 12 5 7	CCXO
3 − 5 7	CO
5 4 5 − 7 − 7 − 8 5 9 7	XXXO
10 6 9 6 10 − 3 − 3 − 5 7	XCCO
7 − 8 3 8 − 8 7	XXO

4 25 10 8 3 3 8 4 − 8 10 8 − 5 6 7	XXO
6 5 12 9 5 9 5 6 − 10 11 7	XO
4 4 − 6 4 4 10 8 4 5 4 7	XO
8 7	O
6 7	O
2 − 4 4 − 7 − 9 6 8 10 9 − 4 7	2XXXO
10 6 6 9 6 12 3 6 6 7	O
9 7	O
4 4 − 7 − 4 7	XXO
7 − 5 9 9 8 6 7	XO
10 4 5 4 11 4 8 7	O
10 3 8 10 − 11 − 7 − 11 − 10 9 7	XXXXO
4 4 − 10 7	XO
12 − 7 − 5 5 − 12 − 3 − 3 − 7 − 5 5 −	BXXBCCX
11 − 7 − 5 6 5 − 5 3 2 9 11 8 9 5 − 6 4 7	XXXXXO
5 6 6 8 7	O
7 − 11 − 11 − 6 7	XXXO
5 6 7	O
3 − 7 − 9 10 7	CXO
9 8 5 5 9 − 5 8 8 9 5 − 7 − 9 8 12 10 7	XXXO
6 10 10 7	O
8 3 4 9 8 − 9 8 10 8 6 8 9 − 4 7	XXO
6 7	O
8 12 5 6 6 8 − 6 4 9 8 5 10 6 − 10 7	XXO
7 − 8 6 5 6 10 8 − 7 − 10 3 8 11 10 − 5 4 7	XXXXO
6 8 4 7	O
7 − 7 − 6 9 7	XXO
3 − 6 8 3 7	CO
4 11 6 5 7	O
6 2 10 6 − 11 − 6 7	XXO
5 9 8 10 10 6 6 7	O
5 12 11 7	O
7 − 9 8 11 7	XO
11 − 3 − 9 9 − 5 7	XCXO
8 6 7	O

```
6 9 8 3 3 8 8 8 11 8 6 — 7 — 3 — 5 7        XXCO
6 6 — 6 3 10 7                              XO
5 5 — 10 9 12 6 12 11 12 6 3 5 10 —         XX
    7 — 7 — 8 11 7                           XXO
5 8 12 4 8 7                                O
6 7                                         O
10 8 6 6 3 7                                O
9 7                                         O
8 9 5 3 9 10 9 10 7                         O
8 6 7                                       O
6 10 11 4 7                                 O
5 9 6 10 4 5 — 11 — 6 3 8 4 8 9 5 8 8 8     XX
    8 3 9 5 3 7                              O
8 6 4 5 9 7                                 O
8 6 8 — 4 10 4 — 6 4 11 2 8 9 5 6 — 7 — 8 9 9 7   XXXXO
9 10 9 — 3 — 11 — 3 — 4 6 6 7               XCXCO
9 2 7                                       O
11 — 6 7                                    XO
9 8 4 8 6 8 7                               O
7 — 10 9 8 8 4 5 5 9 3 6 4 7                XO
5 7                                         O
8 7                                         O
2 — 7 — 6 10 3 11 3 6 — 9 5 8 9 — 10 8 6 7  2XXXO
8 4 5 8 — 5 9 9 10 9 4 9 11 9 8 6 5 — 6 8 9 9 7   XXO
3 — 5 9 11 4 8 4 8 7                        CO
7 — 7 — 10 7                                XXO
10 7                                        O
10 9 10 — 10 11 5 7                         XO
6 6 — 4 7                                   XO
3 — 6 6 — 6 5 8 8 7                         CXO
7 — 2 — 4 7                                 X2O
9 7                                         O
8 4 3 4 10 6 7                              O
7 — 5 7                                     XO
10 8 11 8 11 9 6 11 9 8 5 3 11 8 5 3 8 6 9 7   O
6 5 5 8 4 6 — 11 — 6 6 — 5 10 10 9 8 6 7    XXXO
```

6 8 5 6 − 10 5 4 8 8 5 6 9 9 2 10 − 7 − 5 11 2	XXX
10 10 8 11 8 12 5 − 9 8 4 4 4 6 8 3 6 7	XO
9 7	O
8 3 8 − 2 − 5 8 5 − 5 8 8 8 7	X2XO
10 8 5 7	O
12 − 10 7	BO
11 − 11 − 8 9 2 8 − 10 3 2 6 7	XXXO
8 7	O
6 3 7	O
9 7	O
6 8 10 5 8 8 9 7	O
7 − 7 − 6 8 7	XXO
9 3 8 10 3 9 − 8 10 11 6 11 3 5 5 9 4 7	XO
6 10 9 3 12 5 4 10 8 12 3 10 2 8 2 9 6 − 11	XX
3 − 6 4 8 8 4 10 12 8 5 9 9 7	CO
8 10 4 8 − 5 2 7	XO
9 6 7	O
6 3 6 − 9 10 3 9 − 2 − 7 − 8 7	XX2XO
7 − 5 8 6 3 8 11 7	XO
11 − 7 − 11 − 6 8 10 5 9 8 7	XXXO
9 6 8 12 6 6 8 6 7	O
7 − 6 5 5 11 5 5 10 5 7	XO
5 8 4 3 7	O
10 6 2 12 9 8 6 9 8 7	O
7 − 5 7	XO
7 − 6 7	XO
9 8 12 8 3 4 12 8 10 3 10 7	O
5 8 11 6 6 3 7	O
8 6 4 7	O
6 7	O
11 − 12 − 6 6 − 8 6 4 8 − 4 11 10 10 6 8 7	XBXXO
5 9 5 − 9 8 7	XO
2 − 4 4 − 4 7	2XO
2 − 5 7	2O
7 − 8 6 7	XO
5 12 6 3 6 6 4 11 5 − 12 − 10 10 − 10 7	XBXO
7 − 8 8 − 12 − 7 − 6 10 2 4 7	XXBXO

10 5 8 9 11 10 — 10 1 1 7	XO
8 2 6 3 10 6 7	O
10 5 5 9 7	O
4 7	O
8 9 6 4 4 5 4 7	O
5 7	O
11 — 3 — 7 — 2 — 12 — 8 12 5 7	XCX2BO
11 — 10 8 4 5 6 8 5 5 6 6 5 11 5 7	XO
8 11 8 — 11 — 7 — 7 — 10 12 6 6 9 4 4 10 —	XXXXX
6 10 5 7	O
7 — 5 11 4 10 7	XO
9 12 11 9 — 8 8 — 7 — 4 2 4 — 6 4 11 3 8 8 8 5 7	XXXXO
8 4 10 6 6 7	O
8 5 9 4 3 10 5 2 10 9 8 — 8 9 6 7	XO
12 — 3 — 6 5 10 6 — 11 — 8 2 4 2 11 2 6 8 —	BCXXX
7 — 10 2 8 6 2 7	XO
3 — 10 9 11 11 8 5 5 3 7	CO
5 9 3 11 8 9 6 9 10 7	O
6 11 4 7	O
6 5 8 4 9 2 11 8 7	O
8 11 6 11 7	O
8 10 7	O
6 5 9 10 5 6 — 6 5 8 8 5 4 8 2 8 6 — 6 9 4 8 9 6 —	XXX
5 12 8 12 5 — 5 9 5 — 7 — 4 6 7	XXXO

THE GRI ROULETTE MASTER
- Advanced Winning Roulette Strategy -

Here it is! **Finally**, Gambling Research Institute has released the **GRI Roulette Master**—a **powerful** strategy formerly used only by **professional** and high stakes players. This **strongman strategy** is **time-tested** in casinos and has proven **effective** in Monte Carlo, the Caribbean, London, Atlantic City, Nevada and other locations around the world. It's available here **now!**

EASY TO LEARN

The beauty of the GRI Roulette Master is that it's **easy to learn** and easy to play. Its simplicity allows you to **leisurely** make the **correct bets** at the table, while always knowing exactly the amount necessary to insure **maximum effectiveness**.

BUILT-IN DYNAMICS

Our betting strategies use the **built-in dynamics** of roulette and ensure that only the best bets are working for us. There are no hunches or second guessing the wheel—all you do is follow the instructions, play the necessary bets, and when luck comes your way, **rake in the winnings**.

BUILT-IN SAFEGUARDS

The GRI Roulette Master's **built-in safeguards** protect your bankroll against a few bad spins while allowing you to **win steady sums of money**. Not only does this strategy **eliminate the pitfalls** of other strategies which call for dangerous and frightening bets at times, but also, allows you three styles of betting: **Conservative** for players seeking a small but steady low risk gain: **Aggressive** for players wanting to risk more to gain more: and **Very Aggressive** for players ready to go all out for **big winnings!**

BONUS!!!—Order now, and you'll receive the **Roulette Master-Money Management Formula** ($15 value) **absolutely free!** Culled from strategies used by the top pros, this formula is an **absolute must** for the serious player. It's bound right into the strategy.

To order send just $25 (plus postage and handling) by check or money order to:
Cardoza Publishing, P.O. Box 98115, Las Vegas, NV 89193

BACCARAT MASTER CARD COUNTER
New Winning Strategy!

For the **first time**, GRI releases the **latest winning techniques** for making money at baccarat. This **exciting copyrighted** strategy, played by **big money players** in Monte Carlo and other exclusive locations, is **not available anywhere else.** Based on the same principles that have made insiders and pros **hundreds of thousands of dollars** at blackjack—card counting!

MATHEMATICALLY TESTED
Filled with charts for **easy reference and understanding**. Contains the most thorough mathematical **analysis** of baccarat in print (though explained in terms anyone can understand). You'll see exactly how this strategy works.

SIMPLE TO USE, EASY TO MASTER
You'll learn how to count cards without the mental effort needed for blackjack! No need to memorize numbers—keep the count on the scorepad. Easy-to-use, play the strategy while enjoying the game!

LEARN WHEN TO BET BANKER, PLAYER
No more hunch bets—use the *Baccarat Master Card Counter* to determine **when to bet Player or Banker**. You learn the basic counts (running and true), deck favorability, symmetrical vs. non-symmetrical play, when to increase bets and much **more** in this **winning strategy**.

PLAY SCIENTIFICALLY TO WIN
Drawing and standing advantage, average edge, average gain, total gain, win-loss and % of occurrence are shown for every relevant hand. You won't need to know these numbers or percentages, but we've included them here so you see exactly how the strategy works. You'll be the best player at the table—after just one reading! Baccarat can be beaten. This strategy shows you how!

This copyrighted strategy can only be purchased from Cardoza Publishing

To order send just $50 by check or money order to:
        Cardoza Publishing, P.O. Box 98115, Las Vegas, NV 89193

Win at Blackjack Without Counting Cards!!!
Multiple Deck 1, 2, 3 Non-Counter - Breakthrough in Blackjack!!!

BEAT MULTIPLE DECK BLACKJACK WITHOUT COUNTING CARDS!
You heard right! Now, for the **first time ever**, win at multiple deck blackjack **without counting cards**! Until I developed the Cardoza Multiple Deck Non-Counter (the 1,2,3 Strategy), I thought it was impossible. Don't be intimidated anymore by four, six or eight deck games—for **you have the advantage**. It doesn't matter how many decks they use, for this easy-to-use and proven strategy keeps you **winning—with the odds**!

EXCITING STRATEGY—ANYONE CAN WIN! - We're excited about this strategy for it allows anyone at all, against any number of decks, to have the **advantage** over any casino in the world in a multiple deck game. You don't count cards, you don't need a great memory, you don't need to be good at math - you just need to know the **winning secrets** of the 1,2,3 Multiple Deck Non-Counter and use but a **little effort** to win $$$.

SIMPLE BUT EFFECTIVE! - Now the **answer is here**. This strategy is so **simple**, yet so **effective**, you will be amazed. With a **minimum of effort**, this remarkable strategy, which we also call the 1,2,3 (as easy as 1,2,3), allows you to win without studiously following cards. Drink, converse with your fellow players or dealer - they'll never suspect that you can **beat the casino**!

PERSONAL GUARANTEE - And you have my personal **guarantee of satisfaction**, 100% money back! This breakthrough strategy is my personal research and is guaranteed to give you the edge! If for any reason you're not satisfied, send back the materials unused within 30 days for a full refund.

BE A LEISURELY WINNER! - If you just want to play a **leisurely game** yet have the expectation of winning, the answer is here. Not as powerful as a card counting strategy, but **powerful enough to make you a winner** - with the odds!!!

EXTRA BONUS! - Complete listing of all options and variations at blackjack and how they affect the player. ($5.00 Value!)

EXTRA, EXTRA BONUS!! - Not really a bonus since we can't sell you the strategy without protecting you against getting barred. The 1,000 word essay, "How to Disguise the Fact That You're an Expert," and the 1,500 word "How Not To Get Barred," are also included free. ($15.00 Value)

To order, send ~~$75~~ $50 (plus postage and handling) by check or money order to:
Cardoza Publishing, P.O. Box 98115, Las Vegas, NV 89193

CARDOZA SCHOOL OF BLACKJACK
- Home Instruction Course - $200 OFF! -

At last, after years of secrecy, the **previously unreleased** lesson plans, strategies and playing tactics formerly available only to members of the Cardoza School of Blackjack are now available to the general public - and at substantial savings. **Now**, you can **learn at home,** and at your own convenience. Like the full course given at the school, the home instruction course goes **step-by-ste**p over the winning concepts. We'll take you from layman to **pro.**

MASTER BLACKJACK - Learn what it takes to be a **master player.** Be a **powerhouse,** play with confidence, impunity, and **with the odds** on your side. Learn to be a **big winner** at blackjack.

MAXIMIZE WINNING SESSIONS - You'll **learn how** to take a good winning session and make a **blockbuster** out of it, but just as important, you'll learn to cut your losses. Learn exactly when to end a session. We cover everything from the psychological and emotional aspects of play to altered playing conditions (through the **eye of profitability**) to protection of big wins. The advice here could be worth **hundreds (or thousands) of dollars** in one session alone. Take our guidelines seriously.

ADVANCED STRATEGIES - You'll learn the latest in advanced winning strategies. Learn about the **ten-factor,** the **ace-factor,** the effects of rules variations, how to protect against dealer blackjacks, the winning strategies for single and multiple deck games and how each affects you; the **true count,** the multiple deck true count variations, and much, much more. And, of course, you'll receive the full Cardoza Base Count Strategy package.

$200 OFF - LIMITED OFFER - The Cardoza School of Blackjack home instruction course, retailed at $295 (or $895 if taken at the school) is available here for just $95.

DOUBLE BONUS! - **Rush** your order in **now,** for we're also including, **absolutely free,** the 1,000 and 1,500 word essays, "How to Disguise the Fact that You're an Expert", and "How Not to Get Barred". Among other **inside information** contained here, you'll learn about the psychology of the pit bosses, how they spot counters, how to project a losing image, role playing, and other skills to maximize your profit potential.

To order, send $95 (plus postage and handling) by check or money order to:

Cardoza Publishing, P.O. Box 98115, Las Vegas, NV 89193

THE CARDOZA CRAPS MASTER
Exclusive Offer! - Not Available Anywhere Else)
Three Big Strategies!

Here It is! **At last**, the **secrets** of the **Grande-Gold Power Sweep, Molliere's Monte Carlo Turnaround** and the **Montarde-D'Girard Double Reverse** - three big strategies - are made available and presented for the **first time anywhere**! These powerful strategies are designed for the serious craps player, one wishing to bring the best odds and strategies to hot tables, cold tables and choppy tables.

I. THE GRANDE-GOLD POWER SWEEP (HOT TABLE STRATEGY)
This **dynamic strategy** takes maximum advantage of hot tables and shows you how to amass small **fortunes quickly** when numbers are being thrown fast and furious. The Grande-Gold stresses aggressive betting on wagers the house has no edge on! This previously unreleased strategy will make you a powerhouse at a hot table.

2. MOLLIERE'S MONTE CARLO TURNAROUND (COLD TABLE STRATEGY)
For the player who likes betting against the dice, Molliere's Monte Carlo Turnaround shows how to turn a cold table into hot cash. Favored by an exclusive circle of professionals who will play nothing else, the uniqueness of this strongman strategy is that the vast majority of bets **give absolutely nothing away to the casino**!

3.MONTARDE-D'GIRARD DOUBLE REVERSE (CHOPPY TABLE STRATEGY)
This **new** strategy is the **latest development** and the **most exciting strategy** to be designed in recent years. **Learn how** to play the optimum strategies against the tables when the dice run hot and cold (a choppy table) with no apparent reason. **The Montarde-d'Girard Double Reverse** shows you how you can **generate big profits** while less knowledgeable players are ground out by choppy dice. And, of course, the majority of our bets give nothing away to the casino!
BONUS!!!
Order now, and you'll receive **The Craps Master-Professional Money Management Formula** ($15 value) **absolutely free**! Necessary for serious players and **used by the pros**, the **Craps Master Formula** features the unique **stop-loss ladder**.
The Above Offer is Not Available Anywhere Else. You Must Order Here.
To order send ~~$75~~ $50 (plus postage and handling) by check or money order to:
Cardoza Publishing, P.O. Box 98115, Las Vegas, NV 89193